DEREK PRINCE

DEFEAT
THE
DEVIL

DISMANTLING THE ENEMY'S PLAN
TO DESTROY YOUR LIFE

WHITAKER
HOUSE

DEFEAT THE DEVIL:
Dismantling the Enemy's Plan to Destroy Your Life
(Previously titled *Lucifer Exposed: The Devil's Plan to Destroy Your Life*)

Derek Prince Ministries • P.O. Box 19501 • Charlotte, North Carolina 28219-9501
www.derekprince.org

ISBN: 978-1-64123-910-3 • eBook ISBN: 978-1-64123-911-0
Printed in the United States of America
© 1975, 2006, 2022 by Derek Prince Ministries–International

Whitaker House • 1030 Hunt Valley Circle • New Kensington, PA 15068
www.whitakerhouse.com

The Library of Congress has cataloged the original trade paperback edition as follows:
Prince, Derek.
Lucifer exposed : the Devil's plan to destroy your life / Derek Prince.
p. cm.
ISBN-13: 978-0-88368-836-6 (trade pbk. : alk. paper)
ISBN-10: 0-88368-836-0 (trade pbk. : alk. paper)
1. Spiritual warfare. I. Title.
BV4509.5.P748 2006
235'.47—dc22   2006015718

2 3 4 5 6 7 8 9 10 11 ⨆⨆ 29 28 27 26 25 24 23 22

CONTENTS

INTRODUCTION: THE BATTLE WE FACE

It is a very dangerous situation to have powerful and active enemies working against you and not even be aware that you have those enemies. As Christians, the enemies we face are not persons of flesh and blood; they are invisible spirit beings.

The themes we are going to deal with in this book concern matters that are not discerned by human senses. The Bible speaks about a hidden wisdom that *"eye has not seen, nor ear heard, nor have entered into the heart of man"* (1 Corinthians 2:9). These realities are invisible and spiritual. They are only understood through the Scriptures by the illumination of the Holy Spirit. There is no other source of reliable information.

THE TRUE REALITY

Many people imagine that what we can see, hear, taste, smell, and touch are the only true realities. Down through the ages, however, a number of philosophers have come to the conclusion that what we see, hear, taste, smell, and touch are not truly real; they are temporary, and they are very often deceptive. These philosophers have warned us that we cannot rely only on our senses.

And the Bible agrees! Paul says that the things which are seen are fleeting; the things which are not seen are eternal. (See 2 Corinthians 4:18.) In other words, our sensory world is passing away; therefore, it is only partly real because it does not endure. But the spiritual world that we cannot see, that we cannot perceive with our senses, is the true reality. It alone will endure.

WISDOM AND REVELATION

So, when we come to the theme of invisible enemies, we begin by making a mental adjustment. We have to say to ourselves, "I'm not going to limit myself only to the things that I can see and hear and taste and smell and touch; I'm going to open my heart and mind to the revelation that is recorded in Scripture through the Holy Spirit, and to the reality of a different world."

In essence, this book has to do with two opposing kingdoms at war with one another. They are not natural kingdoms, such as Britain or Sweden or the United States. Rather, they are invisible spiritual kingdoms. One is the kingdom of God and the other is the kingdom of Satan. This is the setting of the battle we face.

Paul prayed that God would give the Ephesian Christians a spirit of wisdom and revelation in the knowledge of Him. (See Ephesians 1:17.) I pray the same for us: that God may grant us wisdom and revelation as we open our hearts to His Word, because we are addressing matters that are made known only through revelation.

Dear Lord, open our hearts and minds to the reality of the spiritual realm and to the very real battle we face as Your children and citizens of Your kingdom. Show us the way to complete victory through the sacrifice of Your Son Jesus and the power of Your Holy Spirit. In Jesus's name, amen.

ONE

OUR INVISIBLE ENEMIES

*"O foolish Galatians! Who has bewitched you that you
should not obey the truth…?"*
—Galatians 3:1

In 1963, the first year I was in the United States, I was invited
to become pastor of a Pentecostal congregation in Seattle,
Washington. I was a bit naive in those days and unaccustomed to many of the normal practices that occur in American
church life. The invitation said that all twelve members of the
board had unanimously agreed to invite me. So, my wife Lydia
and I packed up our belongings and took the journey from
Minneapolis, where we lived at the time, to Seattle.

When we arrived, I discovered that the twelve members
of the board were the only people left who still attended on
Sundays! Furthermore, after just one month, all of them had

resigned except one. My wife and I found ourselves in the midst of extraordinary circumstances. Not long before, this congregation had been filled with several hundred faithful Pentecostals, all of them baptized in the Holy Spirit. They wanted to do right; they were not a bunch of wicked backsliders. When I met them, they were very respectful toward me. But it was as if they were dazed. It didn't matter what I did or said; there was no genuine response. It was a baffling situation.

Lydia was a tremendous woman of prayer. Together, we prayed, "God, You've got to show us what's wrong with these people." The Lord clearly directed me to Galatians 3:1: *"Who has bewitched you…?"* Reading that passage substantially challenged my theology. I thought, "Pentecostals? Tongues-speaking, water-baptized believers—*bewitched?*" This called for further investigation.

I found out that the wife of the previous pastor had fallen in love with one of the board members, and he with her. They engineered a scheme by which the wife divorced the pastor, and the board member divorced his wife. Then the pastor's wife married the board member. The pastor, now her former husband, moved out of the area and, unfortunately, fell away from the faith. His ex-wife became, in effect, the new pastor of the church—until I arrived. This woman seemed to control the congregation just with her eyes. I was told afterward that every time there was an issue in the church, she would say, "Now, how many of you are for me? Put your hand up." Anyone who didn't raise their hand received one of her penetrating stares. She had them mesmerized.

Once Lydia and I had identified the problem, we immediately knew that we were to enter into prayer. As a result, some

WHEN PAUL SAID, *"WHO HAS BEWITCHED YOU...?"* HE WASN'T JUST USING A FIGURE OF SPEECH. PAUL WAS TALKING ABOUT A SPIRITUAL REALITY.

wonderful results took place in that congregation. But the entire experience opened a whole new dimension of the spirit realm to me in a very personal way. When Paul said, *"Who has bewitched you...?"* he wasn't just using a figure of speech. Paul was talking about a spiritual reality.

TWO

OUR MAIN FOE

"You were perfect in your ways from the day you were created, till iniquity was found in you."
—Ezekiel 28:15

In Isaiah 14, we are introduced to a being called Lucifer. In its Latin root, the word *Lucifer* means "the one who brings light." In Hebrew, the word is translated as "the morning star." In any language, Lucifer was portrayed as a radiant, shining, and glorious being. He was what is referred to as an *archangel*. The word *arch*, from its Greek root, means "ruling." The same word occurs in the word *archbishop*, a bishop who rules other bishops. Thus, an archangel is an angel who rules other angels. Lucifer was one of the main archangels, along with Michael and Gabriel,[1] in God's heavenly hosts.

---

1. Biblical references to the archangel Michael: Daniel 10:13, 21; 12:1; Jude 9; Revelation 12:7. Biblical references to the archangel Gabriel: Daniel 8:16; 9:21; Luke 1:19, 26.

LUCIFER'S REBELLION

At some point, however, Lucifer made a grave error. He became so taken with his own glory that he sought to make himself equal with God and turned in rebellion against his Creator.

It is very interesting to compare Lucifer's rebellion with Jesus's obedience. Lucifer was a created being, not equal with God, yet he sought equality with God and fell. Concerning Jesus, Philippians 2 states, *"Who, being in very nature God, did not consider equality with God something to be used to His own advantage"* (verse 6 NIV). Jesus was equal to God, yet He humbled Himself and was ultimately lifted up.

Returning to Isaiah, we see the motivation for Lucifer's rebellion.

> *How you are fallen from heaven, O Lucifer, son of the morning! How you are cut down to the ground, you who weakened the nations!*   (Isaiah 14:12)

Notice how the phrase *"I will"* occurs five times in the next two verses. It exemplifies the will of the creature set up against the will of God.

> *For you have said in your heart: "I will ascend into heaven, I will exalt my throne above the stars of God; I will also sit on the mount of the congregation on the farthest sides of the north; I will ascend above the heights of the clouds, I will be like the Most High."*   (Isaiah 14:13–14)

Lucifer's ambition was to elevate himself to a position of equality with God. He considered himself so wise, so beautiful, and so glorious that he apparently thought to himself, "I could

---

LUCIFER WAS A CREATED BEING,

NOT EQUAL WITH GOD, YET HE

SOUGHT EQUALITY WITH GOD AND

FELL. JESUS WAS EQUAL TO GOD,

YET HE HUMBLED HIMSELF AND

WAS ULTIMATELY LIFTED UP.

---

be God." Scripture suggests that Lucifer undermined the loyalty of one-third of God's angels and drew them with him into his rebellion and into his fall. In response, God said, *"Yet you shall be brought down to hell, to the sides of the pit"* (Isaiah 14:15 KJVER).

A SATANIC RULER

In Ezekiel 28, we get another picture of this same notorious being. The chapter is divided into two sections, each a lamentation or pronouncement of woe. The first section centers on the "prince of Tyre"; the second is about the "king of Tyre." On closer examination, we know that the prince of Tyre was a human being. It is clearly stated that he was a man—even though he claimed to be a god. On the other hand, it is equally obvious that the king of Tyre was no human being.

In this chapter, we are given a glimpse into just how Satan operates. We have a human ruler, the prince of Tyre; but, behind him, in the unseen realm, we have the satanic ruler, the king of Tyre. The human ruler is not much more than a puppet who performs as the strings from the unseen realm dictate his moves. When you begin to understand this truth, history and politics take on a very different meaning. As we examine many of the so-called great and infamous men of history, we begin to see evidence of the strings that guided their movements.

Here is what Ezekiel 28 tells us about Lucifer's original qualities:

> *You were the seal of perfection, full of wisdom and perfect in beauty. You were in Eden, the garden of God; every precious stone was your covering: the sardius, topaz, and*

diamond, beryl, onyx, and jasper, sapphire, turquoise, and emerald with gold. The workmanship of your timbrels and pipes was prepared for you on the day you were created.
(Ezekiel 28:12–13)

It is widely accepted by biblical scholars that Lucifer was responsible for orchestrating the worship of heaven. He was a musical expert and continues to use music as a means of captivating people to this day.

You were the anointed cherub who covers; I established you; you were on the holy mountain of God; you walked back and forth in the midst of fiery stones. You were perfect in your ways from the day you were created, till iniquity was found in you. By the abundance of your trading you became filled with violence within, and you sinned; therefore I cast you as a profane thing out of the mountain of God; and I destroyed you, O covering cherub, from the midst of the fiery stones. (Ezekiel 28:14–16)

Now let us pause for a moment to examine a fascinating word that appears in this passage: "*trading.*" In Hebrew, it means "to go up and down as a talebearer, as an agitator, with secret, underhanded agitation." Today, we might call it *campaigning* or *lobbying.* That is how Lucifer usurped the loyalty of the angels: by going back and forth, declaring, in effect, "Look at me. See how beautiful and intelligent I am? Don't you think I'd make a better ruler than God? And, you know, God doesn't really appreciate you. If you'll join me, I'll give you a much higher position in my kingdom than you have at the present time."

THE FIRST SIN TOOK PLACE
IN HEAVEN, NOT ON EARTH. IT
WASN'T DRUNKENNESS;
IT WASN'T ADULTERY;
AND IT WASN'T EVEN LYING.
IT WAS PRIDE. AND IT IS STILL THE
MOST DEADLY OF ALL SINS.

THE TALEBEARER

Let's look at some other biblical uses of the Hebrew word translated *"trading"* in Ezekiel 28 in order to see the accuracy of applying this description to Satan. The first is from the Lord's admonitions to the Israelites in the book of Leviticus: *"You shall not go about as a talebearer among your people"* (Leviticus 19:16). The root word for *"talebearer"* is the same as the word for *"trading."* This verse describes a slanderer, a person bringing false insinuations and accusations. Lucifer falsely accused God of being a despot, a tyrant who only cared for His own grandeur and glory, with no appreciation for these angels who were so faithfully serving Him.

In Proverbs 11, the same word is used again: *"A talebearer reveals secrets, but he who is of a faithful spirit conceals a matter"* (verse 13). We see a contrast—the opposite of the talebearer is a person *"of a faithful spirit."*

In Proverbs 20, there is another instance of the same word: *"He who goes about as a talebearer reveals secrets; therefore do not associate with one who flatters with his lips"* (Proverbs 20:19). The talebearer and the flatterer are very closely related to one another. In other words, Lucifer flattered these angels into believing that he would give them a much better deal than God was giving them. This is so vivid for me because I have seen flattery in operation many times on the human level in churches and other places. And exactly the same being has been behind such activity throughout history. Flattery and lies are Lucifer's way of doing things.

In Jeremiah 6:28 and 9:4, and Ezekiel 22:9, the description is again accurately translated *slanderer*. It is the same Hebrew word: a talebearer, a slanderer, a person who goes to and fro sowing disaffection and disloyalty by using flattery and misrepresenting authority.

LUCIFER'S PRIDE

Returning to Ezekiel 28, we see precisely what caused Lucifer's downfall.

Your heart was lifted up because of your beauty; you corrupted your wisdom for the sake of your splendor.
(Ezekiel 28:17)

What was Lucifer's initial motivation? What was the first sin? Pride. The first sin took place in heaven, not on earth. It wasn't drunkenness; it wasn't adultery; and it wasn't even lying. It was pride. And it is still the most deadly of all sins. There are scores of churchgoers today who wouldn't dream of committing adultery or getting drunk but who are easily enticed into pride without realizing how dangerous it really is.

The archangel Lucifer was so beautiful, he became proud. The transition from archangel Lucifer to Satan (the adversary of God Almighty) was made complete through his pride.

You defiled your sanctuaries by the multitude of your iniquities, by the iniquity of your trading.   (Ezekiel 28:18)

Lucifer had been responsible for the sanctuary of God in heaven. He was in charge of the worship. He was the cherub who covered the place where God's presence was manifested. He was responsible for the music. He was an artist. He was very accomplished. But then he rebelled, and he fell. Once more, what brought about his demise? Pride!

THREE

THE BATTLE LINES ARE DRAWN

"Now Satan stood up against Israel."
—1 Chronicles 21:1

Lucifer was perhaps the wisest and most beautiful of all God's creatures. But Scripture says his heart was lifted up. (See Ezekiel 28:2–19.) After growing proud because of his wisdom and his beauty, and after hatching his planned rebellion against God, he was cast down from the presence of God. His traitorous angels were cast down with him.

To counteract the effects of Lucifer's rebellion, God devised an alternative plan. Since pride had been the root of Lucifer's rebellion, God's response was to design a different kind of creature—one who was destined to take Lucifer's place. The new creature God fashioned for this purpose was man. Or, as he is referred to in the Hebrew, 'adam, bearing in mind that Adam is not only a proper name but also the name of our race.

GOD'S ALTERNATIVE PLAN

God created Adam as unique from any other creature. There was something special about Adam's mode of creation that was designed in the mind of the Creator to militate against pride. Adam came from a source different from any other created being we know of: the very lowest, the very humblest of materials. Yet God made him capable of becoming the very highest. God combined in Adam both the lowest and the highest.

Here is the description of the creation of Adam in Genesis:

And the Lord *God formed man* [or 'adam] *of the dust of the ground, and breathed into his nostrils the breath of life; and man became a living being* [or "soul" kjv, kjver].

(Genesis 2:7)

For me, this is such a vivid picture—and I believe it took place just the way it is described. I can see the great Creator, the One through whom all things were created as the New Testament reveals. I can see the eternal Son of God, the Word of God, the second person of the Godhead. I can see Him there in that garden, stooping down and, with His divine fingers, molding a perfect figure of clay. Although it was indeed so perfect, it was still just clay. Then, the Creator stooped yet lower. He placed His divine lips against those lips of clay, His divine nostrils against those nostrils of clay, and He breathed into that figure the breath of life.

ADAM CAME FROM A SOURCE
DIFFERENT FROM ANY OTHER
CREATED BEING WE KNOW OF:
THE VERY LOWEST, THE VERY
HUMBLEST OF MATERIALS. YET
GOD MADE HIM CAPABLE OF
BECOMING THE VERY HIGHEST.

FIVE VITAL FACTS

Let me point out five vital facts about the creation of man, or Adam, as revealed in this passage.

1. GOD NAMED HIM

First of all, creation is the first time in the record of Scripture that personal names are introduced. It says, *"The LORD God formed man* ['adam]." "The LORD" (in small caps) is the sacred, personal name of the true God, usually rendered *Jehovah.* Modern scholars say it was probably pronounced *Yahweh.* But here is the important factor to remember: it is a personal name. Likewise, man ('adam) is a personal name. So, a personal God created a personal man for a person-to-person relationship between them. This indicates that the great intent of the Creator was to have fellowship with His creature, person to person.

2. HE STOOPED DOWN

Second, we see that God stooped to create man. He bent in the dust and formed the body. Then He stooped still lower and put His lips against those lips of clay and breathed His divine breath into that body. God had to stoop to create man.

3. HE IMPARTED HIMSELF

Third, God imparted Himself to man. He breathed His very own divine breath into that body of clay.

4. HE BLENDED THE DIVINE AND THE MUNDANE

Fourth, as a result, God combined in man the highest and the lowest—that which was from God Himself directly, and that which was from the earth, the dust. Can you understand something profound about yourself when you consider this? There is something very high and something very low in you. For each of us, a large part of our total experience of life is the conflict between the high and the low.

5. HE OPENED THE WAY FOR FELLOWSHIP

The fifth fact is that man now had the potential for a dual relationship. Through his spirit, that which came from God, man related to God. But through his body, that which came from the earth, man related to the world. So again, we see a truth that is profound in our experience. There is something in us that relates to God, which was made for fellowship with Him—for person-to-person relationship. However, there is also something in us that is very earthly that relates to this world.

Here we have the picture of God's alternative plan. The created archangel had fallen. As a result, in order to undercut the tendency toward pride, God created another kind of being from a different source—the earth—into whom He breathed His own divine life.

SATAN'S COUNTERATTACK

Satan, the already-fallen angel, the enemy of God and of man, retaliated. He had particular enmity against man for two reasons. First of all, he could attack God's image in man. You see, man visibly represented God to the rest of creation. Satan could not touch God Himself. But he could make war against the very image of God within man. His delight was to defile that image, to destroy it, to humiliate it—and to that end, he worked tirelessly.

The second reason Satan had such malice toward man was due to the fact that man was destined to take Satan's place of dominion. From the moment of man's creation, Satan saw him as a rival whom he needed to eliminate.

Ironically, Satan procured man's downfall through the same motivation that caused his own downfall. That process is described in Genesis. In the form of the serpent, Satan came into the garden where God had placed Adam and his wife, Eve, whom God also created. Satan tempted them into disobedience and rebellion. This is the record of that deception and downfall:

> *Now the serpent was more crafty than any of the wild animals the* LORD *God had made. He said to the woman, "Did God really say, 'You must not eat from any tree in the garden'?" The woman said to the serpent, "We may eat fruit from the trees in the garden, but God did say, 'You must not eat fruit from the tree that is in the middle of the garden, and you must not touch it, or you will die.'" "You will not certainly die," the serpent said to the woman. "For God knows that when you eat from it your eyes will be opened, and you will be like God, knowing good and evil."*
>
> (Genesis 3:1–5 NIV)

To our dismay, we are all too familiar with what happened next. Eve was persuaded by the temptation of Satan the serpent, reached out her hand, took the fruit, and convinced her husband to join her in disobedience.

THREE PHASES OF TEMPTATION

I want to point out three specific phases of temptation—the way Satan came against Adam and Eve to entice them to rebel.

Satan's first attack was directed against God's word as He had conveyed it to Adam and Eve. God had said to Adam, *"You must not eat from the tree of the knowledge of good and evil, for when you eat from it you will surely die"* (Genesis 2:17 NIV). Satan's first approach was to question God's word. He said to Eve, *"Did God really say, 'You must not eat from any tree in the garden'?"* (Genesis 3:1 NIV). Satan was too clever to begin with a direct denial, so he began with a subtle question. His motive was to discredit God's word. When Eve entertained the question, he then proceeded to discredit God Himself.

Next, the serpent said to the woman, *"You will not certainly die…. For God knows that when you eat from it your eyes will be opened, and you will be like God, knowing good and evil"* (Genesis 3:4–5 NIV). The thrust of that statement is self-evident. The implication is that God was an arbitrary tyrant who, after creating Adam and Eve, was keeping them in a position lower than what they deserved. Satan implied that God knew they had the potential and ability to become something much higher, but He was keeping them in arbitrary and unreasonable subjection. Having first discredited God's word, Satan then proceeded to discredit God's character. He wanted to give Adam and Eve a false picture of their loving and gracious Creator. He wanted to paint God as an arbitrary despot by discrediting the word of God and the very character of God Himself.

In the third phase, Satan offered to Adam and Eve the very same motivation that had caused his own fall—the prospect of equality with God. He said, *"When you eat from it your eyes will be opened, and you will be like God, knowing good and evil"* (Genesis 3:5 NIV). In effect, he was saying, "You won't need to depend any longer on God. You'll have enough knowledge in

SATAN COULD NOT TOUCH GOD
HIMSELF. BUT HE COULD MAKE
WAR AGAINST THE VERY IMAGE OF
GOD WITHIN MAN. HIS DELIGHT
WAS TO DEFILE THAT IMAGE,
TO DESTROY IT, TO HUMILIATE IT—
AND TO THAT END,
HE WORKED TIRELESSLY.

yourself that you'll be equal with Him." That was exactly the same temptation that impelled his fall: *"I will make myself like the Most High"* (Isaiah 14:14 NIV). Now he was saying to Adam and Eve, "You will be like God. This position of subjection and dependence that you're in isn't worthy of you. You're capable of a higher destiny. Reach up and reach out for knowledge that will set you free from this slavish dependence on your Creator."

It is very clear that Adam's sin was a carbon copy of Satan's rebellion. Both Satan and Adam had been created on a level that was blessed, appointed, and ordained by God. But, through pride, they both reached up for equality with God. And reaching up, they both fell. Remember, *"Whoever exalts himself will be humbled"* (Luke 14:11).

FOUR

GOD'S SOLUTION

*"For Christ also suffered once for sins, the righteous for the
unrighteous, to bring you to God."*
—1 Peter 3:18 (NIV)

How would God now respond to the fall of Adam? In creating man, God stooped to the dust, but in the transition from creation to redemption, God stooped still lower. God's answer to pride is always humility. The more God encounters pride, the more He Himself displays humility.

Man had fallen. He was alienated, a rebel. God did not abandon him. (Thank God for that.) In the person of Jesus Christ, God stooped to the lowest level. He identified Himself with the fallen race and expiated its guilt. Then, to crown it all, He exalted these fallen, but redeemed, creatures to the highest place in the universe, continually demonstrating an immutable principle: "The way up is down."

TOTAL IDENTIFICATION

Let's look at some Scriptures that speak, first of all, about how Christ identified Himself with the human race and extinguished its guilt.

> *Since the children have flesh and blood, He too shared in their humanity so that by His death He might break the power of him who holds the power of death—that is, the devil—and free those who all their lives were held in slavery by their fear of death.* (Hebrews 2:14–15 NIV)

Earlier, I pointed out that when Adam rebelled, instead of becoming a king, he became a slave—a slave of Satan, a slave of corruption, a slave of death. He was no longer free. But in order to deliver him from that slavery, Jesus took upon Himself the Adamic nature, the form of humanity, though without its sin. To share in humanity, He took upon Himself the same flesh and blood you and I have. Why is this so significant? Because by His death, Jesus would destroy the one who holds the power of death (the devil) and free all of us who were held in slavery to the fear of death.

A REDEMPTIVE ACT

What Jesus achieved was a total identification. To redeem all humans, Jesus took upon Himself the nature of man, the fallen creature. This is stated, too, in 1 Peter:

THROUGH FAITH AND REPENTANCE,
WE CAN BE IDENTIFIED WITH
CHRIST—IDENTIFIED NOT ONLY IN HIS
DEATH BUT ALSO IN HIS SUBSEQUENT
EXALTATION. THIS IS THE GREAT
MYSTERY OF IDENTIFICATION; FIRST,
CHRIST WITH US; THEN WE, THROUGH
FAITH, WITH CHRIST.

"He Himself bore our sins" in His body on the cross, so that we might die to sins and live for righteousness; "by His wounds you have been healed." (1 Peter 2:24 NIV)

On the cross, Jesus became totally identified with our sin, our guilt. He Himself became the last great guilt offering that took away the sin and guilt of the human race. He bore our sin. He bore our punishment. Our wounds became His wounds. And He died our death. He eliminated that guilt of rebellion as our representative—the last Adam, hanging on the cross, shedding His lifeblood, giving Himself totally to redeem us.

And then the simple statement:

For Christ also suffered once for sins, the righteous for the unrighteous, to bring you to God. (1 Peter 3:18 NIV)

That is total identification. The righteous took the place of the unrighteous, of the rebel, the alien, the one who had turned against God. He died the death that was our due, to deliver us from the fear of death and to reconcile us to God.

A FURTHER STEP

As we look further, beyond Christ's identification with us, we find that, in turn, through faith and repentance, we can be identified with Christ—identified not only in His death but also in His subsequent exaltation. This is the great mystery of identification; first, Christ with us; then we, through faith, with Christ.

But because of his great love for us, God, who is rich in mercy, made us alive with Christ even when we were dead in transgressions—it is by grace you have been saved. And

God raised us up with Christ and seated us with Him in the
heavenly realms in Christ Jesus. (Ephesians 2:4–6 NIV)

Our redemption is the other side of the coin, the complementary side of identification. First, Jesus identified Himself with us, the fallen race. He took our place. He paid our penalty. He died our death. He expiated our guilt. Then, recognizing these facts and, in turn, identifying ourselves with Him in faith, we are identified with Him in all that follows His death.

That passage in Ephesians 2 states three great steps of our identification with Jesus: (1) God made us alive with Christ; (2) God raised us up (resurrected us with Christ). But it doesn't stop there. (3) God seated us with Him in the heavenly realm. Christ is seated on a throne; God seated us with Him. He has enthroned us with Christ. Notice those three upward steps of our identification with Jesus: made alive with Him, resurrected with Him, and enthroned with Him. It is the same immutable principle: the way up is down. We go from the lowest to the highest.

Amazingly, God has made us, creatures who were fallen but then redeemed and raised up, His eternal demonstration to the whole universe that God exalts the lowest to the highest. Please do not miss this important principle, which runs through the story of redemption. It is not just a matter of history. It is a matter of the outworking of a universal law: Whoever humbles himself will be exalted, and whoever exalts himself will be humbled. (See again Luke 14:11.) The way up is down.

FIVE

ONE SACRIFICE

"[Jesus] *Himself bore our sins in His own body*
on the tree, that we, having died to sins,
might live for righteousness."
—1 Peter 2:24

The sacrificial death of Jesus on the cross is the only basis of God's provision for every need of the whole human race. Instead of God doing a lot of different actions at different times, Scripture says, *"By one offering* [sacrifice] *He has perfected forever those who are being sanctified"* (Hebrews 10:14). The writer of Hebrews explained that after Jesus had offered that one sacrifice, He *"sat down at the right hand of God"* (verse 12). Why did He sit down? Because He was never going to have to do it again.

DELIVERED FROM DARKNESS

Through the cross, Jesus administered to Satan and his kingdom a total, permanent, irreversible defeat. Jesus will never have to do that work again. Satan has already been defeated. You and I do not have to do the foundational work to defeat Satan. But we must apply the victory that Jesus has already won and walk in that victory.

> *Giving thanks to the Father who has qualified us to be partakers of the inheritance of the saints in the light.*
> (Colossians 1:12)

Our inheritance is in the light, and there is no darkness whatsoever in it. It is totally in the light. How has God done it?

> *He has delivered us from the power* [I prefer to say "domain"] *of darkness and conveyed* [translated] *us into the kingdom of the Son of His love, in whom we have redemption through His blood, the forgiveness of sins.*
> (verses 13–14)

So, by redemption through the blood of Jesus, we have been delivered from the domain of darkness and translated, or carried over, into the kingdom of the Son of God's love.

A CHANGE OF DOMAIN

The word that is translated as *domain* or *power* is actually the normal Greek word for "authority." In speaking of *domain* or *power*, it is very important for us to understand that Satan has authority. Why does he have authority? Because he is the ruler of all those who are in rebellion against God. Anyone who is in

THROUGH THE CROSS, JESUS ADMINISTERED TO SATAN AND HIS KINGDOM A TOTAL, PERMANENT, IRREVERSIBLE DEFEAT. YOU AND I DO NOT HAVE TO DO THE FOUNDATIONAL WORK TO DEFEAT SATAN. BUT WE MUST APPLY THE VICTORY THAT JESUS HAS ALREADY WON AND WALK IN THAT VICTORY.

rebellion against God is automatically under the authority of Satan. He is in the "domain of darkness."

> *And you He* [God] *made alive, who were dead in trespasses and sins....*   (Ephesians 2:1)

That is not physical death. That is spiritual death, and it applies to all of us. That's where all of us were. We were all dead to God because we were living in trespasses and sins.

> *...in which you once walked according to the course of this world, according to the prince of the power of the air....*
>   (verse 2)

WHICH REALM?

Satan is the ruler with authority in the region of the air. There are two Greek words for "air." One of them gives us the English word *ether*. The other gives us the English word *air*. The difference in Greek is as follows: *ether* is the higher, rarer atmosphere; *aer* (*air* in English) is the lower atmosphere, contiguous with the earth's surface. The word used here refers to the second meaning. Satan is the ruler of the realm of authority of the earth's surface, contiguous with the earth. The remaining part of that passage in Ephesians states that he is...

> *...the spirit who now works in the sons of disobedience....*
>   (Ephesians 2:2)

Why does he have the power to work in those people? Because they are disobedient to God. We have only two options: we can be either in Satan's territory or in God's territory. There is no third option. If we are submitted to God's appointed Ruler, Jesus, then we have the right to be in God's kingdom. If we have rejected God's appointed Ruler, Jesus, then we are in Satan's kingdom because we have become sons of disobedience. Satan has legitimate authority over all those who are in rebellion against God. Regardless of their denomination or affiliation, Satan rules over all rebels.

> *...among whom also we all once conducted ourselves in the lusts of our flesh, fulfilling the desires of the flesh and of the mind....* (Ephesians 2:3)

"*We all*" did this. All of us. Notice also that our errors were not just of the flesh. Our minds also were alienated from God. Scripture says the carnal mind is enmity toward God. (See Romans 8:7.) You have an enemy of God dwelling in your cranium: the carnal mind.

Continuing in Ephesians 2, we read:

> [We] *were by nature children of wrath, just as the others.* (verse 3)

This is a very important statement. We were born with a disobedient nature. It is a fact of human experience. How many parents ever had to train their children to be naughty? Not one, because in every descendant of Adam, there is the nature of a rebel. Adam did not have any children until he was a rebel. Consequently, everyone who descended from Adam has inherited the nature of a rebel. This nature makes us subject to the authority of Satan.

SIX

THE WAY OUT

*"But now in Christ Jesus you who once were far off have
been brought near by the blood of Christ."*
—Ephesians 2:13

God offers a way out of Satan's kingdom and into God's
kingdom. I have a vivid picture in my mind of what this way
is like. Some years ago, I was preaching in a remote area in the
country of Zambia, right by the Zambezi River, which, at that
point, separated Zambia from Zaire. I had a congregation of
about four or five hundred Africans, and I was trying to com-
municate to them this wonderful fact that God has made it possible for us to escape from the kingdom of Satan and enter the
kingdom of God. I said to them, "Suppose, here on the east side
of the Zambezi River, we are in the kingdom of darkness. But
on the other side of the river is the kingdom of light. In order

to get from the kingdom of darkness into the kingdom of light, we need to have a bridge across the river." Then I added, "God has provided a bridge. There is only one bridge—the cross of Jesus Christ. By taking that bridge, you can cross over from the kingdom of darkness to the kingdom of the Son of God's love."

OUR DESTINATION

God doesn't simply want us to stay on the bridge. He wants us to move into His kingdom and rule with Jesus as kings and priests. (See, for example, Revelation 1:6.) That is our destination. Here is the problem with the Christian church: we have millions and millions of people who have left the kingdom of darkness, but they are still hanging around on the bridge. They have never moved fully into the kingdom of God. Many people say, "I'm saved, and that's it." Well, it is wonderful to be saved, but that is not the end. The bridge is just the way from one kingdom to the other.

The New Testament teaches that through redemption by the blood of Jesus, God has made us kings and priests in the here and now, in His kingdom.

> *Those who receive abundance of grace and of the gift of righteousness will reign in life now through the One, Jesus Christ.*   (Romans 5:17)

Let me ask you a direct question: Where are you right now? Are you hanging around on the bridge? Or are you reigning in life with Jesus? Everyone believes they will reign in the next life. That is wonderful, but it is not what God is concerned about right now. He is concerned about where we are in this life.

THERE IS ONLY ONE BRIDGE FROM THE KINGDOM OF DARKNESS TO THE KINGDOM OF LIGHT—THE CROSS OF JESUS CHRIST. BUT GOD DOESN'T SIMPLY WANT US TO STAY ON THE BRIDGE. HE WANTS US TO MOVE INTO HIS KINGDOM AND RULE WITH JESUS AS KINGS AND PRIESTS.

POWERS AND PRINCIPALITIES

It is very important for us to see how Jesus accomplished what He accomplished.

> *Having disarmed principalities and powers, He* [Jesus] *made a public spectacle of them, triumphing over them in it.*   (Colossians 2:15)

What principalities and powers did He disarm through the cross? Who is represented by the word *"them"*? If your answer is "Satan and his minions," you are correct. Other translations (NASB, for example) identify *"rulers and authorities"* as the ones Jesus disarmed on the cross.

> *For we do not wrestle against flesh and blood, but against principalities, against powers* [notice the same words as in Colossians 2:15], *against the rulers of the darkness of this age, against spiritual hosts of wickedness in the heavenly places.*   (Ephesians 6:12)

I am privileged to have studied Greek since I was ten years old. (Actually, it wasn't always a privilege, believe me!) But I am qualified to teach it at the university level. That does not mean I am always right, but at least I am entitled to my informed opinion. (In actuality, nobody is always right about the Greek language; it is historically a very complicated language.) Please let me offer you the "Prince version" of the verse that talks about wrestling against flesh and blood: "For our wrestling match is not against persons with bodies...."

We are not fighting persons with bodies. We are in a wrestling match with a very powerful and highly organized kingdom that has rulers, sub-rulers, and sub-sub-rulers. Each ruler is responsible to Satan for a certain area under his authority. Satan has the whole world divided up into territories that he seeks to dominate through these rulers. To continue the "Prince version" of Ephesians 6:12: "...against the world dominators of this present darkness."

I deliberately use the word *dominators* here because the Greek word is very strong, and because domination is characteristically a satanic activity. God never dominates, so if you encounter domination, you can be sure you are not dealing with God. I refer to the powers we deal with as "the world dominators of this present darkness." Satan's aim, which he is steadily and consistently pursuing, is to become the ruler of this world.

One place we see this clearly is in reference to the end times. As I understand prophecy pertaining to that time, there will be a very short period right at the end of the age when Satan will temporarily succeed. He will do so through a certain man whom he will raise up, called the Antichrist, one whom he himself will empower. Satan will persuade much of the world (those whose names are not written in the Lamb's Book of Life) to worship the Antichrist. In worshipping him, they will actually be worshipping Satan who empowered him.

SATAN'S AIM

Why does Satan want, above all things, to be worshipped? Because of his desire to be equal with God, which was the cause of his fall. Today, Satan is not on the level he experienced before his fall, but he still has one way to claim equality with God—through worship. That is the one activity which, by right, belongs only to God. But if Satan can receive worship, it affirms his claim to be equal with God.

When we become truly aware of the conflict between the kingdoms, we find that Satan's supreme ambition is to be worshipped. It is also very important to realize that what we worship has power over us. I have ministered to people who have worshipped Satan. Believe me, to get them free is a major battle. Why? Because Satan feels he has legitimate power over them.

The final description of this satanic kingdom in Ephesians 6:12 is *"spiritual hosts* [or forces] *of wickedness in the heavenly places."* Satan's headquarters are not in hell; they are in the heavenlies. Some of the traditional language in the church does not correspond with Scripture on this matter. To people who say Satan is in hell, I reply, "It would be nice if it were true, but it isn't." Satan is very much at large in the world today. Peter wrote this warning: *"The devil walks about like a roaring lion, seeking whom he may devour"* (1 Peter 5:8).

SEVEN

WHAT JESUS ACCOMPLISHED

"For Christ is the end of the law for righteousness
to everyone who believes."
—Romans 10:4

Let us now examine the fact that Jesus disarmed the principalities and powers of Satan. He stripped them of all their weapons. The Greek is very emphatic. He left them nothing. How did He do it?

THE GUILT FACTOR

First, we need to understand that Satan's primary weapon against the human race is guilt. Jesus stripped him of the ability to make us guilty. Let's examine the facts that we know. God had already dealt with Satan before He created Adam. Satan was already a fallen angel, the enemy of God and anything that God created—particularly man. Satan then succeeded in tempting Adam into the same rebellion that he had chosen. In his temptation, Satan said, "You shall be like God," which was exactly what had first motivated his own fall.

Let us assume that Satan knows a lot about God's feelings and attitudes, and he knows of God's love for the human race. We read in the book of Job that when the angels came to appear before God, Satan came among them. (See Job 1:6.) At that time, he still had some access to the presence of God. Furthermore, the text seems to indicate that the only one who spotted Satan was the Lord, because Satan had transformed himself into an angel of light.

I imagine the dialogue between Satan and God might have gone like this:

Satan says to the Lord, "You're a righteous God. You're a just God, and I'm a rebel. I know it. I've got no doubt about it. See that lake of fire over there, with all the unpleasant smoke coming out of it? I know that's where I'm headed. I know it was created for me and for my angels. But, God, I just want to remind You of something. You see these men and women whom You love? They're as guilty as I am. They're rebels too. So, when You throw me and my angels into that lake, You're going to have to throw them into that lake as well. Just remember, God, Your justice makes it essential."

GOD'S PLAN

I suppose we might imagine that for centuries God didn't answer Satan. But God had His plan. His plan was Jesus. When Jesus came, He became the last Adam, the final representative of the Adamic race. He took upon Himself all the guilt and all the condemnation and all the evil consequences of Adam's transgression. He died as the last Adam, He was buried as the last Adam, and He rose again as "the second man," the head of a new race.

In that way, Jesus extinguished the guilt of Adam's race. For those who believe in Jesus, the guilt of Adam is no longer held against them. As a result of Jesus's sacrifice, God can now forgive us without compromising His justice. He has removed Satan's argument from him by the death of Jesus. He has made it possible for us to be received by God as righteous without any condemnation.

REMOVING THE BARRIER

If we look briefly in Colossians, we will see how Jesus removed our guilt:

And you, being dead in your trespasses and the uncircumcision of your flesh, He has made alive together with Him, having forgiven you all trespasses, having wiped out the handwriting of requirements that was against us, which was contrary to us. And He has taken it out of the way, having nailed it to the cross. (Colossians 2:13–14)

Through the death of Jesus, without compromising His justice, God can forgive us all our past acts of disobedience. How many of them? All of them. If even one sin were left unforgiven, we would have no right of access to God. Thankfully, God has made it possible for us to be assured that all our past sinful acts have been forgiven.

AS A RESULT OF JESUS'S
SACRIFICE, GOD CAN NOW FORGIVE
US WITHOUT COMPROMISING
HIS JUSTICE. HE HAS REMOVED
SATAN'S ARGUMENT FROM HIM
BY THE DEATH OF JESUS. HE HAS
MADE IT POSSIBLE FOR US TO BE
RECEIVED BY GOD AS RIGHTEOUS
WITHOUT ANY CONDEMNATION.

For He Himself [Jesus] *is our peace, who has made the two*
[Jew and Gentile] *one and has destroyed the barrier, the
dividing wall of hostility, by setting aside in His flesh the
law with its commands and regulations.*

(Ephesians 2:14–15 NIV)

Nothing could be clearer than that. Jesus abolished the law
with its commandments and regulations.

*Therefore by the deeds of the law no flesh will be justified in
His* [God's] *sight, for by the law is the knowledge of sin.*

(Romans 3:20)

In actual fact, we are justified, but not by keeping the law. As
this Scripture attests, no human being will achieve righteousness in the sight of God by keeping the law. The problem isn't
with the law; the problem is with us. We can't keep it. And we
can't split the law up into a lot of different sections and say, "I'll
keep Section A and ignore Sections B and C. I'll keep Section
D and then I'll keep a few other sections."

The law is one law. You either keep it all—perfectly—all
the time, or you do not achieve righteousness by it. There is no
other option.

*For sin shall not have dominion over you, for you are not
under law but under grace.*   (Romans 6:14)

Notice that *law* and *grace* are mutually exclusive alternatives.
If we are under law, we can't be under grace. If we are under
grace, we can't be under law. We can't have it both ways at the
same time. If we are under law, Paul says, sin *will* have dominion
over us. If we are under grace, sin *will not* have dominion over us
because we are not under law.

LIVING IN FREEDOM

For as many as are led by the Spirit of God, these are sons of God.   (Romans 8:14)

How do we live as sons and daughters of God? By being led by the Holy Spirit. This essential truth has escaped the notice of most Christians. We talk about being saved, baptized in water, baptized in the Spirit, and that's it. But these aspects are only the beginning. Life is being led by the Spirit daily, hourly, moment by moment.

For Christ is the end of the law for righteousness to everyone who believes.   (Romans 10:4)

If we believe, then, for us, Christ is the end of the law for righteousness. Not the end of the law as part of God's Word. Not the end of the law as part of the history of the culture of Israel. But it is the end of the law as a means of achieving righteousness with God.

This is true for everyone who believes: Jew or Gentile, Protestant or Catholic. It makes no difference. If we are reckoned righteous before God by the death of Jesus, it means the end of the law.

But if you are led by the Spirit, you are not under the law.   (Galatians 5:18)

We can choose one or the other, but we can't have it both ways. Jesus has made it possible for us to be guiltless and not condemned. He has abolished the law as a means of achieving righteousness with God. As long as we are seeking to achieve righteousness by keeping a law, we will never be without

HOW DO WE LIVE AS SONS AND DAUGHTERS OF GOD? WE TALK ABOUT BEING SAVED, BAPTIZED IN WATER, BAPTIZED IN THE SPIRIT, AND THAT'S IT. BUT THESE ASPECTS ARE ONLY THE BEGINNING. LIFE IS BEING LED BY THE SPIRIT DAILY, HOURLY, MOMENT BY MOMENT.

condemnation. We can never be sure we have done enough. We can never be sure that before each day ends, we will not have broken some aspect of the law.

I am not suggesting we should be lawless or disobedient. What I am saying is we will never achieve righteousness with God by keeping a set of rules. To try to do that is to insult God, because we are telling Him, in effect, "Jesus didn't need to die. I could have made it without Him." What a terrible thing to say: that the death of Jesus wasn't necessary.

So, we are set free from condemnation on the basis of these two facts. First, our past sins can be totally forgiven—*all* of them. Second, we are not required to observe a set of rules to achieve righteousness with God.

EIGHT

ENFORCING THE VICTORY

"That you may be able to withstand in the evil day, and having done all, to stand."
—Ephesians 6:13

In the matter of spiritual warfare, Christ has clearly won the victory. However, He leaves it to us to enforce that victory. It is very important that we understand this. If we had to win the victory, we could never do it. It is a good thing for us that we don't have to. Jesus said, "I have won the victory." (See, for example, 1 Corinthians 15:57.) Once again, it is our task to enforce the victory He has won.

EXERCISING AUTHORITY

We see this principle after the resurrection when Jesus appeared to His disciples and said:

All authority in heaven and on earth has been given to Me.
Therefore go and make disciples of all nations.
(Matthew 28:18–19 NIV)

It is clear that Jesus has obtained the authority. We have to exercise the authority. In a sense, His authority is inoperative until we exercise it.

The only way the world can ever fully understand what Jesus has accomplished is for us to exercise His authority on His behalf, making disciples of all nations. This is a clear scriptural principle. Jesus has accomplished it; we have to apply it.

There are two mistakes we must be careful not to make. The first is thinking that we have to win the victory. We don't have to because Jesus has won the victory. The second mistake is thinking there is nothing left for us to do. That is not true either. We have to take steps to apply the victory that Jesus has won.

The first step we must take is to put on the whole armor of God. In Ephesians 6, where Paul speaks about the kingdom of Satan in the heavenlies, he immediately follows with this:

Therefore take up the whole armor of God, that you may be able to withstand in the evil day, and having done all, to stand. (Ephesians 6:13)

Notice, we must "take it up." The armor does not grow on us. Neither does God place it on us. We have to put it on ourselves. Paul was writing to people who were Christians—much like you and me—and he assigned *them* the responsibility of taking up the armor.

THE ONLY WAY THE WORLD CAN

EVER FULLY UNDERSTAND WHAT

JESUS HAS ACCOMPLISHED IS FOR

US TO EXERCISE HIS AUTHORITY

ON HIS BEHALF, MAKING

DISCIPLES OF ALL NATIONS.

WEAPONS OF WARFARE

First of all, let us look in 2 Corinthians, where Paul is addressing all Christians. This is not just written to apostles or pastors. It applies to every Christian.

> *For though we walk in the flesh, we do not war according to the flesh.*   (2 Corinthians 10:3)

Paul states that while we live in physical bodies, we are involved in a war. But the war is not in the physical realm. If, then, the war is not in the physical realm, it must be in the spiritual realm.

> *For the weapons of our warfare are not carnal but mighty in God for pulling down strongholds [or fortresses], casting down arguments and every high thing that exalts itself against the knowledge of God, bringing every thought into captivity to the obedience of Christ.*
>   (2 Corinthians 10:4–5)

Where the *New King James Version* says *"arguments,"* other versions say *"reasonings"* (YLT) or *"speculations"* (NASB95). We also find the words *"knowledge"* and *"thought"* used in this verse. If we examine those five words—*arguments, reasonings, speculations, knowledge,* and *thought*—we recognize they all belong to the same realm: the mind. This is a vital fact. The battlefield is the mind. That is where the battle is fought. Anyone who has tried to live the Christian life has discovered this, I am sure. We may not always recognize it as a theological fact, but the truth of the matter is clear: most of our battles are in our minds.

Another point we must consider about our warfare, remembering that we are all in it, is that our kingdom is at war with

Satan's kingdom. We are citizens of the kingdom of God; therefore, we are at war with Satan and his kingdom.

THE NATURE OF STRONGHOLDS

The weapons God has given us are mighty for pulling down strongholds or fortresses. (See 2 Corinthians 10:4.) Whose fortresses are we pulling down? Satan's. And in what realm? The realm of the mind.

Satan builds many different fortresses in people's minds. But if I were to choose one word to sum them all up, it would be the word *prejudice*. Prejudice means having your mind made up before you know the facts. The typical statement of the prejudiced person is, "My mind is made up; don't confuse me with the facts!" In its variety of forms, prejudice is one of the most powerful strongholds of Satan. He builds prejudice as a fortress in people's minds to prevent the truth of the gospel from entering and doing its work.

We see this clearly in regard to people involved in cults and false religions. A believer can quote the Bible perfectly to them, but they can't hear because their minds are totally preprogrammed. They will have a specific way to answer you. And that represents a fortress in their minds that prevents the truth of God's Word from entering.

This is also clear in encounters with Muslims. Even though they may believe certain truths about Jesus (even admitting that He was the Messiah or agreeing He was born of a virgin), there are two truths they will never admit. First, that Jesus died on the cross. Mohammed taught that an angel spirited Jesus away before He died. Second, they will passionately oppose that

THE WEAPONS GOD HAS GIVEN US
ARE MIGHTY FOR PULLING DOWN
STRONGHOLDS OR FORTRESSES.
(SEE 2 CORINTHIANS 10:4.) WHOSE
FORTRESSES ARE WE PULLING
DOWN? SATAN'S. AND IN WHAT
REALM? THE REALM OF THE MIND.

He is the Son of God. These are the two major strongholds in the Muslim mind, and they are very powerful strongholds. A Muslim may go a long way in his interest in Jesus, but when he is asked to acknowledge that Jesus is the Son of God, a wall comes up. Only supernatural weapons can demolish that wall.

NINE

OUR SPIRITUAL WEAPONS

"Therefore take up the whole armor of God...."
—Ephesians 6:13

Let us now consider some of the weapons of our warfare that are described in Ephesians:

> *Therefore take up the whole armor of God, that you may be able to withstand in the evil day, and having done all, to stand. Stand therefore, having girded your waist with truth, having put on the breastplate of righteousness, and having shod your feet with the preparation of the gospel of peace; above all, taking the shield of faith with which you will be able to quench all the fiery darts of the wicked one. And take the helmet of salvation, and the sword of the Spirit, which is the word of God; praying always with all prayer and supplication in the Spirit.* (Ephesians 6:13–18)

THE BELT OF TRUTH

A phrase used quite often in the Bible is "Gird up your loins." To understand this concept, we need to realize that in Bible days, both men and women wore long garments that extended below their knees. In order to do anything active, a person first had to get those long garments up above their knees for free movement of their legs. To accomplish this, the person put on a belt, pulled up the long garment, and tucked it into the belt. After that, they were ready for action. Unless someone did this, they couldn't go into action because the long garment would have impeded them.

How does this apply to us? I believe the "long garments" that encumber us can be religious language and behavior. We must be ruthlessly honest with ourselves and, as the Holy Spirit leads, with other people. We cannot encumber ourselves with religious clichés. They are a terrible hindrance if we want to be truly committed Christians. We cannot hide behind religious talk; we have to be sincere.

THE BREASTPLATE OF RIGHTEOUSNESS

The area of the body the breastplate protects is the heart. I have always been blessed by this statement of Solomon:

Watch over your heart with all diligence, for from it flow the springs of life.   (Proverbs 4:23 NASB)

What we have in our hearts will ultimately determine the course of our lives, for good or for evil. That is why it is essential that we protect our hearts from all kinds of evil and why Paul speaks about the breastplate of righteousness as a protection of the heart.

WHAT WE HAVE IN OUR HEARTS
WILL ULTIMATELY DETERMINE THE
COURSE OF OUR LIVES, FOR GOOD
OR FOR EVIL. THAT IS WHY IT IS
ESSENTIAL THAT WE PROTECT OUR
HEARTS FROM ALL KINDS OF EVIL
AND WHY PAUL SPEAKS ABOUT THE
BREASTPLATE OF RIGHTEOUSNESS
AS A PROTECTION OF THE HEART.

Paul returns to this theme of armor in another epistle and calls it *"the breastplate of faith and love"* (1 Thessalonians 5:8 NASB). He describes the breastplate from another point of view.

If we put these two passages together, *"the breastplate of righteousness"* is a *"breastplate of faith and love."* This tells us the kind of righteousness Paul has in mind. Not the righteousness of works; not the righteousness of a religious law; but the righteousness that comes only by faith.

THE SHOES OF THE GOSPEL

For this item of armor identified as *shoes*, I prefer to say "the boots of the preparation of the gospel of peace." Roman soldiers wore leather boots that were strapped all the way up the calf. These boots were firmly fixed on them.

Scripture emphasizes that we must have our boots on. We have to be prepared to bring the message of the gospel of peace. The fact is, if we don't have peace in our own hearts, we really don't have much to transmit to others. We must believe and know the Scriptures. We must be able to point people to the truth of God's Word. This is the preparation of the gospel of peace.

THE SHIELD OF FAITH

We see two kinds of shields spoken of in the New Testament: one is a small, round shield; the other is a long, oval shield that could cover the whole person. The shield spoken of in this passage is the long, oval shield behind which a man could be totally covered. This is the shield of faith.

THE HELMET OF SALVATION

What area of the person does the helmet protect? The mind. Because of my own struggles with depression, God showed me early on that I had to learn to protect my mind. When I asked Him how to do this, the answer came from the Word of God: the helmet of salvation.

When God made that truth clear to me, I said to myself, "I know I'm saved. Does that mean I already have the helmet of salvation?" The answer came when I saw that, in this passage, Paul is talking to people who have been saved and baptized in the Spirit. Yet he still tells them to take up the helmet of salvation. We don't automatically have the helmet because we are saved. Clearly, we need to "put it on."

In 1 Thessalonians, we find a very useful cross-reference: *"And as a helmet the hope of salvation"* (1 Thessalonians 5:8). It helped me greatly to discover that the nature of the helmet is *hope.* Just as faith protects our hearts, hope protects our minds against depression and discouragement.

Biblical faith is in the realm of the heart: *"With the heart one believes..."* (Romans 10:10). But hope is in the realm of the mind. The writer of Hebrews says, *"Faith is the substance of things hoped for"* (Hebrews 11:1). So, on the basis of faith in the heart, we may have hope in the mind. And hope safeguards our minds.

THE SWORD OF THE SPIRIT

In the list of spiritual armor, there is one more item of equipment: the sword of the Spirit—the Word of God. Perhaps you are already familiar with the erudite distinctions between *logos* and *rhema*—*logos* being the eternal counsel of God and *rhema* being the Word of God spoken. This citation in Ephesians 6 tells us that the sword of the Spirit is the *rhema* of God. In other words, it is not the Bible on your bedside table; it is the Word of God operating when you speak it with your mouth.

The spoken Word is a sword, and that is how Jesus used it when Satan confronted Him in the wilderness. Three times, He said, *"It is written."* (See Matthew 4:1–11; Luke 4:1–13.) That is making the written Word, *logos*, your *rhema*; and that is what drives Satan back.

THE SEVENTH WEAPON

When we analyze this list of six items of equipment, we see that they are essentially defensive weapons—all except the sword, which is an offensive weapon. Even so, we need to realize that a sword can only operate as far as our arm can reach. We cannot cast down Satan's kingdom without additional weapons.

Whenever I find six of a good thing in the Bible (this is just my personal observation), I tend to look for the seventh. So, as we examine the list of these six items, we need to look for the seventh. I believe the seventh weapon is presented at the end of the passage: *"Praying always with all prayer and supplication in the Spirit"* (Ephesians 6:18).

Prayer is our means of breaking out of the restrictions of reaching only as far as our arm will extend. Prayer is limitless. It is our "intercontinental ballistic missile." We can launch it from anywhere and make it land anywhere.

In the weapon of prayer, there are three main components to do the job: the Word of God (the *logos*); the name of Jesus; and the blood of Jesus.

PRAYER IS OUR MEANS OF BREAKING

OUT OF THE RESTRICTIONS OF

REACHING ONLY AS FAR AS OUR ARM

WILL EXTEND. PRAYER IS LIMITLESS.

IT IS OUR "INTERCONTINENTAL

BALLISTIC MISSILE." WE CAN

LAUNCH IT FROM ANYWHERE AND

MAKE IT LAND ANYWHERE.

Even though prayer is one of our most powerful weapons, we need a means to launch it. Missiles require a means for launching. Any bomb requires a means to drop it. Any bullet requires a means to fire it. In the old days, any arrow required a bow to shoot it. I want to suggest again that the same is true of the weapon of prayer. It requires some means of "launching" it.

Remember that in regard to the seventh weapon against Satan's kingdom, we have the main components of the weapon: the Word of God, the name of Jesus, and the blood of Jesus. How do we get them to be operative against the kingdom of Satan? It is my experience that we have to make use of our four main ways to launch that seventh weapon: *prayer, praise, preaching,* and *testimony.*

But these four launching devices are only effective insofar as they are loaded with the Word of God, the name of Jesus, and the blood of Jesus (the primary components of the weapon of prayer).

OUR NEED FOR GOD'S POWER

Out of the mouth of babes and nursing infants You [God] have ordained strength, because of Your enemies, that You may silence the enemy and the avenger.　　(Psalm 8:2)

Who is *"the enemy and the avenger"*? Satan. Who are the other enemies? Satan's kingdom, principalities, and powers in the heavenlies.

We must realize our need for God's supernatural power. Christianity is a religion of the supernatural. I once read through the book of Acts, examining it to see what would happen if I removed all references to the manifestly supernatural. (Not just inward supernatural experiences but actions that are visible—that can be perceived by the senses.) At the end of my study of the book of Acts, which has twenty-eight chapters, I discovered that not one chapter out of the twenty-eight would be left intact if we eliminated the supernatural.

The only record we have in Scripture of how the church is intended to operate attests that we cannot function effectively and accomplish the will of God solely by our own natural ability. We must have the supernatural enabling of the Holy Spirit. And one main form of that enabling is the list of supernatural gifts of the Holy Spirit in the twelfth chapter of 1 Corinthians.

This statement by the apostle Paul summarizes what I am saying: *"For the kingdom of God is not in word but in power"* (1 Corinthians 4:20).

It is not a matter of theology, although theology certainly has its place. It is not a matter of argument. It is not a matter of intellectual proof. It is the demonstration of the supernatural power of God.

I believe supernatural power is the primary need of the church today, especially when we are surrounded by millions of Muslims. Nothing will reach the Muslim mind more effectively than the demonstration of the supernatural power of God. And today we have an unprecedented opportunity. Instead of our having to go to the Muslims, they have come to us.

In the past, we could not go to their nations and proclaim the gospel because we would have been put in prison or executed. But God has arranged for Muslims to come here. The question is, what is the church doing about it? It is time for the church to rise up and declare, "We will demonstrate to them that Jesus is alive."

TEN

THE CLIMAX OF THE BATTLE

*"The accuser of our brethren, who accused them before our
God day and night, has been cast down."*
—Revelation 12:10

As we conclude our observations about our role in the war
between the kingdom of God and the kingdom of Satan, let
us look at the prophetic climax of this war from the book of
Revelation:

> *And war broke out in heaven: Michael and his angels
> fought with the dragon; and the dragon and his angels
> fought, but they did not prevail, nor was a place found for
> them in heaven any longer. So the great dragon was cast out
> ["that old snake"—that's the Prince version], called the
> Devil and Satan, who deceives the whole world.*
>
> (Revelation 12:7–9)

This passage gives us the most complete description of Satan in one verse. The word *"Devil"* (*diabolos* in Greek) means "a slanderer" or "a false accuser." *"Satan"* means "an enemy" or "an opposer." He is the slanderer who opposes God, the people of God, and the purposes of God while deceiving the whole world.

THE MOMENT OF VICTORY

In the above passage, the great dragon is cast out of his kingdom in the heavenlies. The following verse is not only the climax of the war but also the description of us winning. That is why it is so important.

> *Then I heard a loud voice saying in heaven, "Now salvation, and strength, and the kingdom of our God, and the power [or authority] of His Christ have come, for the accuser of our brethren, who accused them before our God day and night, has been cast down."*   (Revelation 12:10)

In this verse, it is the angels who are talking, and when they say *"our brethren,"* they are talking about us. So, what is Satan doing right now? Accusing us. Where? Before the throne of God. That is a shocking fact, isn't it? And Satan is doing this accusing day and night. His sole purpose is to prove us guilty. (Just as a side note, we cannot truly defeat him until we know how to deal with his weapon of guilt.)

THE MOST POWERFUL SECRET

I will now share what I consider to be the most powerful secret of Scripture that God has ever revealed to me. I regard this as extremely valuable:

And they overcame him by the blood of the Lamb and by the word of their testimony, and they did not love their lives to the death.   (Revelation 12:11)

Notice that this verse says, *"They overcame him."* Who is *"they"*? That refers to us. Who is *"him"*? Satan. Clearly, this is a direct conflict between the church and Satan.

Remember that testimony was one of the four ways of launching the weapons. This means we overcome Satan when we testify personally to what the Word of God says the blood of Jesus does for us. Our testimony makes it personal. It takes the general truth of the Scripture and applies it personally to our lives.

In order to apply this weapon effectively, we have to know what the Word of God says about the blood of Jesus. Otherwise, it won't have impact. Let us examine some of the statements of Scripture about the blood of Jesus.

REDEMPTION

By the blood of Jesus, we are redeemed:

In Him [Jesus] *we have redemption through His blood.*
                                            (Ephesians 1:7)

Redemption means we have been bought back. We were in the kingdom of Satan; we have been bought back out of the kingdom of Satan. The price of our redemption, the apostle Peter tells us, was not silver or gold, but *"the precious blood of Christ, as of a lamb without blemish and without spot"* (1 Peter 1:19).

Let the redeemed of the LORD say so, whom He has redeemed from the hand of the enemy.   (Psalm 107:2)

We make this our personal testimony by saying, out loud, "Through the blood of Jesus, I am redeemed out of the hand of the devil." Why don't you take a moment right now to repeat those words out loud?

CLEANSING

By the blood of Jesus, we are cleansed:

If we walk in the light as He is in the light, we have fellowship one with another, and the blood of Jesus Christ His Son cleanses us from all sin.   (1 John 1:7)

The words used in this passage are all in the continuing present tense: if we continually walk, we continually have fellowship, and the blood continually cleanses us. Bear in mind, it is conditional. If we are not walking in the light, the blood does not cleanse us. But by walking in the light, we have fellowship with our fellow believers. If we are out of fellowship, we are out of the light. If we are out of the light, the blood doesn't cleanse us. That is an important truth to remember.

We make this personal by saying, out loud, "While I am walking in the light, the blood of Jesus is cleansing me, now and continually, from all sin." Why not make this your proclamation as well, right now?

JUSTIFICATION

By the blood of Jesus, we are justified:

Having now been justified by His blood.   (Romans 5:9)

Justified means "acquitted, not guilty, made righteous, just-as-if-I'd never sinned."

WE OVERCOME SATAN WHEN WE
TESTIFY PERSONALLY TO WHAT
THE WORD OF GOD SAYS THE
BLOOD OF JESUS DOES FOR US. OUR
TESTIMONY MAKES IT PERSONAL.
IT TAKES THE GENERAL TRUTH OF
THE SCRIPTURE AND APPLIES IT
PERSONALLY TO OUR LIVES.

We make this our personal testimony (feel free to do it now) by saying, out loud, "Through the blood of Jesus, I am justified, acquitted, not guilty, made righteous, just-as-if-I'd never sinned."

SANCTIFICATION

By the blood of Jesus, we are sanctified:

> *Therefore Jesus also, that He might sanctify the people with His own blood, suffered outside the gate.* (Hebrews 13:12)

Sanctified has both a negative and a positive meaning. Negatively, it means "to be separated and set apart from sin." Positively, it means "to be made a partaker of God's holiness."

We make this our personal testimony by saying (right now), out loud, "Through the blood of Jesus, I am sanctified, separated from sin and the kingdom of Satan, and made a partaker of God's own holiness."

Now let us put these powerful testimonies all together and say them as a personal declaration:

> Through the blood of Jesus, I am redeemed out of the hand of the devil. While I'm walking in the light, the blood of Jesus is cleansing me, now and continually, from all sin. Through the blood of Jesus, I am justified, acquitted, not guilty, made righteous, just-as-if-I'd never sinned. Through the blood of Jesus, I am sanctified, set apart from sin and Satan's kingdom, and made a partaker of God's holiness.

Once we have made this declaration, there is only one reasonable additional response to make: we thank Him. To end this chapter, let's thank the Lord together right now—for His redemption, cleansing, justification, and sanctification.

ELEVEN

THE POWER OF THE CROSS

*"For the message of the cross is foolishness
to those who are perishing, but to us who are being saved
it is the power of God."*
—1 Corinthians 1:18

Over the last few chapters, I have explained the absolute perfection of the redemptive work of Jesus on the cross. His sacrifice has covered every need that could ever arise in our lives. It was a perfect work. Through this work on the cross, Jesus administered a total, eternal, irrevocable defeat to Satan and his kingdom. This is the good news of God's kingdom!

What could we suppose would be the devil's response to this work? What would he want to do about it? He would do his best to undermine the work of the cross. Even more than that, he would do his best to obscure the work of the cross, because once the work of the cross was obscured, he could reassert his control over humanity. And that is precisely what the devil has done and is doing still. Clearly, one of his primary aims is to obscure what was accomplished by the death of Jesus on the cross.

WHY SATAN OBSCURES THE CROSS

We see three reasons for the devil's fierce efforts to nullify the power of the cross. First, the cross is the only basis of all God's provision for His redeemed people. There is no other basis.

> *For by one offering* [sacrifice] *He* [God] *has perfected forever those who are being sanctified.*   (Hebrews 10:14)

By the sacrifice of Jesus on the cross, God has done all that will ever be needed for any human being in any period of history. It is all accomplished through the cross.

Our appropriation of the work of the cross is a process: we *are being* sanctified. What Jesus has done is perfect, finished, complete. But, again, our appropriation is progressive. I don't believe any one person, myself included, has yet appropriated all that has been made available to us through the cross.

As we go through the process of sanctification—being made holy, being conformed to God, thinking God's thoughts, living His way—we will appropriate more and more of God's provision. But if the enemy moves in to obscure the power of the cross, although we should be living as children of the King, we will begin living like beggars and paupers. Our enemy's goal is to obscure the fact that all the benefits God has provided come to us solely on the basis of the cross. Satan is very astute. He knows exactly what to strike at. He knows that if he can neutralize the cross, he has the church at his mercy.

AS WE GO THROUGH THE PROCESS

OF SANCTIFICATION—BEING

MADE HOLY, BEING CONFORMED

TO GOD, THINKING GOD'S

THOUGHTS, LIVING HIS WAY—

WE WILL APPROPRIATE MORE AND

MORE OF GOD'S PROVISION.

The second reason the enemy wants to obscure the power of the cross is that it was the means of Satan's total defeat. In previous chapters, we looked closely at God's redemptive work. Through the cross, Jesus ministered a total, eternal, irreversible defeat to Satan. Satan cannot change that. But what he can try to do is conceal that fact from us. The result would be that we no longer live in victory because we don't comprehend the victory that was won for us.

The third reason Satan obscures the power of the cross is that it is the only source of power for real Christian living. Some Christians and popular psychologists are fond of quoting the Sermon on the Mount as the way people ought to live. As good as that sermon is, the only way we obtain the ability to live in the manner it describes is through the sacrifice of Jesus on the cross.

Jesus's sacrifice dealt with the old man, the fleshly nature. As Paul says, *"Our old man was crucified with Him"* (Romans 6:6). In Galatians, he adds, *"Those who are Christ's have crucified the flesh with its passions and desires"* (Galatians 5:24). Until we learn to apply the cross to our carnal nature, that nature will master us. We cannot master it.

In Romans 6:6, Paul further explains, *"Our old man was crucified...that we should no longer be slaves of sin."* That is the provision of the cross. And once we grasp what Jesus accomplished on the cross in our lives, the devil is defeated.

SATAN'S "FIFTH COLUMN"

In 1936, there was a civil war in Spain between people with two opposing political ideologies. Tragically, the Spaniards were fighting against one another. At one point, a certain Spanish general was besieging a Spanish city. He was asked by a second general, "What is your plan to take this city?" The first general replied, "I have four columns advancing on the city: one from the north, one from the south, one from the east, and one from the west." Then he paused and said, "But it's my fifth column I'm expecting to take the city for me." The second general asked, "Where is your fifth column?" And he replied, "Inside the city." The fifth column is that which is inside, working from within against the people who are unaware of its presence.

That is Satan's tactic to destroy the church. He has never been able to defeat the church from the outside. But once he infiltrates with a fifth column inside, then he can say, "It is my fifth column that will take the city."

In a sense, Satan's deceptive power, especially manifested in the form of witchcraft, is that fifth column inside the church. In Galatians, Paul deals with this very theme, and, in essence, it is the theme of the whole letter. We see this clearly in Paul's words at the beginning of the third chapter of Galatians:

> *O foolish Galatians! Who has bewitched you that you should not obey the truth, before whose eyes Jesus Christ was clearly portrayed among you as crucified?*
>
> (Galatians 3:1)

Let us focus on that rather strange question: *"Who has bewitched you…?"* As we will see in the following verses, these Galatians had been saved and baptized in the Holy Spirit. They had seen God working miracles among them. Nonetheless, they were bewitched. What is my point? The fact that we have been saved, have been baptized in the Spirit, and have experienced miracles is no guarantee that we will not be bewitched by the deceptive power of the enemy—in a word, *witchcraft*.

But how did Paul know that witchcraft was operating? What was the evidence? The answer is very important and revealing. Witchcraft had obscured the revelation the Galatians had received of Jesus Christ crucified. In line with all we have seen in this chapter, the supreme aim of witchcraft in the church has been to hide the reality of Jesus Christ crucified.

FAITH OR THE LAW?

Paul's series of rhetorical questions and their answers in the following verses are also very revealing for us:

> *This only I want to learn from you: Did you receive the Spirit by the works of the law, or by the hearing of faith?*
>
> (Galatians 3:2)

Notice that the Galatians had received the Holy Spirit. Paul was asking them, "How did you receive the Spirit—by keeping the law of Moses or by hearing the gospel with faith?"

> *Are you so foolish? Having begun in the [Holy] Spirit, are you now being made perfect by the flesh? Have you suffered so many things in vain—if indeed it was in vain? Therefore He who supplies the Spirit to you and works miracles among you, does He do it by the works of the law, or by the hearing of faith?*
>
> (Galatians 3:3–5)

The root problem for the Galatians was that the reality of Jesus Christ crucified had been obscured by an evil, satanic power that had moved in. The two problems that resulted were carnality and legalism. The Galatians had gone back to fleshly

THE GALATIANS HAD GONE BACK TO FLESHLY ATTEMPTS TO DO THE WILL OF GOD, TO PLEASE HIM. THEY HAD REVERTED TO KEEPING ALL SORTS OF RULES AS A WAY OF ACHIEVING RIGHTEOUSNESS WITH GOD. BY DOING SO, THEY HAD MISSED THE PURPOSE OF CHRIST'S DEATH.

attempts to do the will of God, to please Him. They had reverted to keeping all sorts of rules as a way of achieving righteousness with God. By doing so, they had missed the purpose of Christ's death. Paul states the final result this way:

> For as many as are of the works of the law are under the curse; for it is written, "Cursed is everyone who does not continue in all things which are written in the book of the law, to do them." (Galatians 3:10)

Essentially, Paul is saying, "If you have gone back to trying to achieve righteousness by keeping the law, remember, you have to keep the *whole* law *all* the time, or you are under a curse." When Israel came into the land of Canaan, one of the first steps they had to take was to pronounce a curse upon themselves if they did not keep the whole law all the time.

We must realize that keeping a little bit of the law some of the time does not do us any good. If we are going to be justified by keeping the law, we have to keep the whole law all the time. And none of us, in God's sight, can ever be justified by the works of the law. Such an idea is a deception of Satan, one that appeals primarily to human pride.

Years ago, when I was in the British Army and came to know Jesus Christ, I became a witness for the Lord. Because I lived a life that was very different from my fellow soldiers, many of them asked what had happened to me. They joked that I had "gotten religion." I told them, "No, I did not get religious. I got saved." Then I would tell them about salvation. Amazingly, the first reaction of almost everyone I talked with was to give me a little list of the rules they kept. Each one seemed to have a list tailored to his own particular life. In other words, the first reaction of man confronted with God's demand for righteousness is, "I'll keep a law." I have said the following words in many places, and sometimes I have shocked Christians with them: "Christianity is not a set of rules!" Once we reduce it to that, we have lost the vision of the cross. And if that happens, we have lost the power of God.

LETHAL LEGALISM

Once again, the two marks of the work of witchcraft in the Galatian church were legalism and carnality. Wherever we encounter legalism, somewhere behind it is witchcraft. Legalism is the greatest single threat to the purposes of God. Some would say the greatest threats are immorality and carnality. But, as a matter of fact, legalism actually promotes those two activities.

How can that be so? If we are always telling people, "You must not lust," and that is all we give them, what happens? We are actually feeding lust. Paul says, *"I would not have known sin except through the law. For I would not have known covetousness unless the law had said, 'You shall not covet'"* (Romans 7:7). Negative rules operate in the area of the flesh, and they feed the very behaviors they are supposed to prevent.

Many individuals feel that if we don't make enough rules, we won't keep people under control. Well, they make fifteen rules, and the people are not under control; so, they make thirty rules, and people are still not under control. So then, they make sixty rules. But the more rules you create in order to make people good, the more you feed the carnal nature, and the carnal nature is incapable of producing anything good.

The book of Galatians, whose themes we have been exploring, is very interesting among all of Paul's epistles. Galatians is the only epistle in which Paul does not begin by thanking God for the people he is writing to. When he wrote to the Corinthian church, even though there was drunkenness at the Lord's Table, incest, and other immorality, Paul still began by thanking God for the grace He had given to that church.

But when Paul writes to the Galatians, he is so worked up, he does not give any thanks. Instead, he begins by saying, *"I marvel that you are turning away so soon from Him who called you in the grace of Christ, to a different gospel"* (Galatians 1:6). What was the problem? Legalism. Paul viewed it as a much greater threat than immorality or drunkenness (not that we would ever suggest to condone those activities).

TWO ASPECTS

Let me now offer a more complete definition of legalism. There are two aspects to this definition. First of all, legalism is attempting to achieve righteousness with God by observing a set of rules. We know God has deemed this method unacceptable as a means of justification. He has said, *"By the works of the law no flesh shall be justified"* (Galatians 2:16). It is impossible.

Second, legalism is adding extra requirements to what God has stated for achieving righteousness with Him. The requirements for achieving righteousness with God are very simply stated in Romans: if you believe in Him who delivered Jesus our Lord to death for our offenses, and raised Him again from the dead for our justification, you are righteous. (See Romans 4:22–25.)

There is no other way to achieve righteousness with God. Nothing else can be added. No person, no church, no group, no preacher has the authority to add any other requirement to achieving righteousness with God than those that are stated in the New Testament.

To sum up, legalism is either attempting to achieve righteousness with God by observing a set of rules or adding to the requirements God has stated in the New Testament.

TWELVE

THE NATURE OF WITCHCRAFT

"For rebellion is as the sin of witchcraft, and stubbornness
is as iniquity and idolatry."
—1 Samuel 15:23

In the above words spoken by the prophet Samuel to King Saul, Samuel makes two comparisons, addressing two very sinful attitudes: rebellion and stubbornness. His statement reveals God's evaluation of them both. Rebellion is a twin of witchcraft; stubbornness is a twin of idolatry.

A STUBBORN PROBLEM

First, let us consider stubbornness. The verse says stubbornness is a form of idolatry. How does that occur? The stubborn person makes idols out of his own opinions. In that light, it is very interesting to consider various attitudes in the church today. Generally, we will not accept drunkards or openly immoral people. But how many stubborn people do we have in church? In God's eyes, they are idolaters.

In most churches, if somebody came in with a wooden idol, fell down, and worshipped it in front of everyone, we would not tolerate that. But, alas, we tolerate a lot of stubborn people, and often we let them get away with it. In God's sight, they are idolaters.

THE ROOT ISSUE

Let us now focus more intently on rebellion. The verse indicates that the root of witchcraft is rebellion. Wherever you find rebellion, you can anticipate witchcraft. I learned this in the ministry of deliverance. For instance, I discovered that if a person needed deliverance from a spirit of witchcraft, almost invariably, they also needed deliverance from rebellion. And conversely, where I would encounter a spirit of rebellion, I would check to see if there was not also a spirit of witchcraft. They are closely related.

Rebellion rejects God's legitimate authority, just as King Saul rejected the authority of God's Word. (See 1 Samuel 15:23.) We cannot exist for long in life without authority. So, if we don't have legitimate authority, illegitimate authority will fill the void. Where we have illegitimate authority, it will be supported by wrongful power. The illegitimate power that supports rebellion is the power of witchcraft. Basically, wherever we find illegitimate authority being exercised, we need to be prepared to deal with witchcraft.

IN MOST CHURCHES, IF SOMEBODY CAME IN WITH A WOODEN IDOL, FELL DOWN, AND WORSHIPPED IT IN FRONT OF EVERYONE, WE WOULD NOT TOLERATE THAT. BUT, ALAS, WE TOLERATE A LOT OF STUBBORN PEOPLE, AND OFTEN WE LET THEM GET AWAY WITH IT. IN GOD'S SIGHT, THEY ARE IDOLATERS.

We see a very clear example of this in the United States in the 1960s. Young people turned their backs on almost all accepted forms of authority—parents, church, government—and they became a generation of rebels.

Over the years, I have dealt with many of those "rebels," and many of them who met the Lord are my friends today. But almost without exception, those who went into rebellion also went into the occult, the satanic supernatural, and witchcraft. This is the logic of spiritual experience. It is almost impossible to be deeply involved in rebellion without sooner or later coming under the power of witchcraft.

CAUSE AND EFFECT

If we go back for a moment to the example of King Saul from 1 Samuel 15, we remember that he disobeyed Samuel's injunction to slaughter all the animals that had been captured from the Amalekites. Instead, he kept *"the best"*—as he called it—to offer to God. God said, in effect, "I am not interested in your sacrifice, because it comes out of disobedience." (See verses 9–23.)

As king of Israel, Saul had actually banished all the witches from Israel. (See 1 Samuel 28:3.) But just before his death—when he could not hear from God—he himself sought a witch out of desperation. (See verse 7.) This was not an accident; it was a matter of cause and effect.

I want to emphasize this point: wherever there is rebellion, sooner or later there will be witchcraft. Let me also emphasize one other point: when you deal with witchcraft (the satanic supernatural, the occult in all its forms), if you only deal with the occult, you have not dealt with the root, because the root of witchcraft is rebellion.

A WORK OF THE FLESH

Witchcraft has two aspects: a natural aspect and a supernatural aspect. Many people do not realize that witchcraft is listed in Scripture as a work of the flesh. It is a characteristic of the fallen human nature.

> *Now the works of the flesh are evident, which are: adultery, fornication, uncleanness, lewdness, idolatry, sorcery, hatred, contentions, jealousies, outbursts of wrath, selfish ambitions, dissensions, heresies, envy, murders, drunkenness, revelries, and the like....* (Galatians 5:19–21)

The King James Version uses the term *"witchcraft"* instead of *"sorcery."* Regardless of which version you use, you have the same meaning: witchcraft is a work of the flesh. That means it is an expression of the unregenerate nature of fallen man. It is what naturally comes out of our fleshly nature.

In our fallen nature, we desire to control people. We desire to get people to do what we want them to do. Very often, we use illegitimate means to make that happen.

THREE EXPRESSIONS OF WITCHCRAFT

The operation of witchcraft involves three key components. When these three activities are happening, whether you realize it or not, it is an encounter with witchcraft. The three key words are *domination, manipulation,* and *intimidation.* The end purpose is control—the need to *dominate.* To achieve this domination, depending on the situation, a person will either use *manipulation* or *intimidation.*

Remember, this is in the natural; we are not talking about anything supernatural yet. Witchcraft, as a work of the flesh, operates in every area of society. Let me give you a few examples.

Whether people like it or not, God has ordained a certain structure in the family. The husband is identified as the head of the wife. (See Ephesians 5:23.) Regardless of modern society's attempts to stand the family on its head, God has not changed the order. Beneath the authority of husband and wife are the children, who, in God's order, are subject to the authority of their parents. Witchcraft will operate in that context through either manipulation or intimidation to set aside the divinely authorized order.

Let's take children first. Children can be manipulators at a very early age. A child of five can learn to use manipulation. Suppose a mother is hosting guests and serving cookies. Her small child knows that her mother does not want her to have any cookies. But she also knows that when guests are present, it is very difficult for Mother to say no. So, while the guests are there, she comes in and says, "Mama, may I have a cookie?" You can guess what the mother will do. She will probably give in. When that happens, she has been manipulated.

Witchcraft can be found in mothers and fathers too. The most common way for witchcraft to operate in a woman is manipulation. In a man, it is intimidation. But each of them has the same aim: to control the other.

So, if the wife does not get her way, she throws a tearful fit, withholds affection, and makes her husband's life miserable. In the end, what does he do? He gives in.

THE OPERATION OF WITCHCRAFT

INVOLVES THREE KEY COMPONENTS.

WHEN THESE THREE ACTIVITIES ARE

HAPPENING, WHETHER YOU REALIZE

IT OR NOT, IT IS AN ENCOUNTER WITH

WITCHCRAFT. THE THREE KEY WORDS

ARE *DOMINATION*, *MANIPULATION*, AND

INTIMIDATION. THE END PURPOSE IS

CONTROL—THE NEED TO *DOMINATE*.

With the husband, it can happen just as frequently, but he may be a brute, a strong man with a bad temper. If he does not get his way, he shouts and becomes violent and threatens, and the whole family tiptoes around him. The one thing they want to avoid is another fit of temper by Daddy. What is he doing? He is intimidating them. His aim is to get his own way.

It can well be that a husband and wife will have differences. The divine order is that they talk it out face-to-face, and prayerfully seek God. But manipulation never faces the real issues. It always goes behind. The real issues are never brought out into the light. Millions of married couples never really bring their differences out into the open. Instead, each tries to go behind the other to get what he or she wants. That is manipulation.

BIBLICAL EXAMPLES OF WITCHCRAFT

Two biblical examples of people using witchcraft on a leadership level are Delilah and Jezebel. In the case of Delilah, although Samson was the strong man of the Bible, Delilah was stronger yet. Scripture tells us Delilah pressed upon Samson; she cried; she had moods. She said to him, "You don't really love me. You haven't told me your secret." Ultimately, Delilah wore him down. (See Judges 16:4–22.) I believe there are few men strong enough to deal with witchcraft in a woman. Very few. I have seen men who exercise strong leadership as the president and CEO of an organization. However, when it comes to dealing with a wife, they are manipulated.

The other example from Scripture is Jezebel. She was by no means a sweet woman. But she knew how to get her husband, King Ahab, to do what she wanted. In reality, she took over ruling Israel, reinforcing the principles we discussed earlier:

usurpation and illegitimate authority. It is interesting that, in Revelation 2, Jezebel is referred to as being inside the church. The New Testament warns us that witchcraft is going to infiltrate the church, and, in many instances, we can see it already.

WITCHCRAFT IN THE CHURCH

There are many examples of manipulation in the church. Let's take a typical Pentecostal congregation, for instance. A young pastor in his first pastorate has about a hundred people in the congregation. He is a little bit nervous and timid. In his congregation, there are two very spiritual sisters. Not just spiritual, but super-spiritual, and they know how the church ought to be run.

Rather than sitting down prayerfully and talking it over with the pastor, one of them gets a "message in tongues," and the other comes up with the "interpretation." Between them, through this method, they end up telling the pastor what to do. What is that? Manipulation.

ENTERTAINING THE THIEF

So, we see that witchcraft as a work of the flesh has three trademarks: domination, manipulation, and intimidation. Wherever you encounter these activities, behind them is the power of witchcraft.

When your eyes are opened to this reality, it is much easier to deal with it. These are real and relevant issues I am talking about. They are not occurring in some other country or on some other planet. They are happening all around us—in the church, in our homes, and in our families.

Witchcraft never came to do any of us any good. Remember that Jesus said, "*The thief does not come except to steal, and to kill, and to destroy*" (John 10:10). If you entertain the thief, you can expect him to do exactly those three things.

THIRTEEN

WITCHCRAFT'S SUPERNATURAL ASPECT

"Now it happened, as we went to prayer, that a certain
slave girl possessed with a spirit of divination met us."
—Acts 16:16

We have seen that witchcraft is a work of the flesh. Now let's explore the fact that witchcraft is not merely a work of the flesh but also an evil, spiritual power.

I believe this was the power that had moved into the Galatian church. What we are talking about is something supernatural. It is more than just human ability. We must recognize that not all supernatural manifestations come from God. Many of them come from Satan.

There are, I believe, only two sources of the supernatural available to men: God or Satan. Any supernatural power that does not come from God does, in fact, come from Satan.

God's kingdom is a kingdom of light. In God's kingdom, we are aware of whose we are, and we know what God is doing because it occurs "in the light." But Satan's kingdom is a kingdom of darkness. In that kingdom, we are not aware of what is manipulating us, what is controlling us, what is driving us, because it occurs "in the darkness."

THREE BRANCHES

There are three main branches of the supernatural aspect of witchcraft as described in the English language. They are (1) witchcraft, (2) divination, and (3) sorcery. These areas cover the whole field of the satanic supernatural, and I will describe each one and provide scriptural examples of them.

1. WITCHCRAFT

Witchcraft is the *power branch*. Its product is power, and it operates through such activities as spells and curses. Perhaps the single most powerful weapon of witchcraft is cursing, which is a very old practice.

In Numbers 22, we find the story of Balaam, who was what we might call a witch doctor. Balaam was hired because he was a good curser. That was his profession.

In verse 10, Balaam is actually explaining to God the proposition he received from Balak:

> *Balak the son of Zippor, king of Moab, has sent to me, saying, "Look, a people has come out of Egypt, and they cover the face of the earth* [speaking of Israel]. *Come now, curse them for me; perhaps I shall be able to overpower them and drive them out."*   (Numbers 22:10–11)

THERE ARE ONLY TWO SOURCES

OF THE SUPERNATURAL

AVAILABLE TO MEN: GOD OR

SATAN. ANY SUPERNATURAL

POWER THAT DOES NOT COME

FROM GOD DOES, IN FACT, COME

FROM SATAN.

This was standard practice in the pagan cultures of the Bible. It was normal for kings or others going to war not merely to fight on the natural plane but to make war on the supernatural plane as well. They would get their witch doctor to curse their enemy. (There exists a list of curses pronounced by the Egyptian pharaohs in the nineteenth century BC against sixty-six different nations.) It was an attempt to bring them to a place where they could be defeated in war.

When Goliath came against David, he cursed him in the name of his gods. (See 1 Samuel 17:43.) That was not just a display of vulgarity. He was actually making this assertion: "My gods can deal with your God."

In a certain sense, ancient warfare was not just a conflict between nations. It was viewed as a test of power between the gods of those nations. For instance, when God dealt with Egypt and brought Israel out, the Bible says that He judged the gods of Egypt—not just the natural rulers but also the spiritual rulers. (See Exodus 12:12; Jeremiah 43:12; Psalm 135:5–10; 82:1.)

Psalm 135:5 says, *"I know that the LORD is great, that our Lord is greater than all gods"* (NIV).

2. DIVINATION

The second branch we will examine is divination; in most modern translations, it is called "fortune-telling." Divination is the *knowledge branch* of witchcraft. The product is not power but knowledge, which, as I pointed out, first led man into sin. The scriptural example in Acts 16 is very clear, describing what happened when Paul and Silas first arrived to preach the gospel in Philippi:

Now it happened, as we went to prayer, that a certain slave girl possessed with a spirit of divination met us.

(Acts 16:16)

The Greek actually says "having a spirit of python" or "a python spirit"; in other words, it was a snake spirit. Remember, snakes have always been regarded in pagan society as the source of unusual knowledge and wisdom.

Significantly, what this girl said was absolutely true. She did not know it by natural means; she knew it by supernatural means. She was just a simple slave girl who had this ability. But she *"brought her masters much profit by fortune-telling"* (Acts 16:16). (Because she was a slave, the profit did not go to her. It went to her masters.)

This girl followed Paul and us, and cried out, saying, "These men are the servants of the Most High God, who proclaim to us the way of salvation." (verse 17)

Again, the amazing fact is that what she said was absolutely true. In the past, I have commented that in contemporary missions, such a young lady might have been made a charter member of the church. She was the first person to recognize who Paul and Silas really were. Yet Paul knew that she was not speaking by God's Spirit but by a divining spirit, a fortune-telling spirit. In the end, he turned around and commanded that spirit to come out of her in the name of Jesus. When it came out, she was no longer able to tell fortunes. Her masters were so angry at the profits they would lose that they brought Paul and Silas before the magistrates; and the rest, as they say, is history. (Read the remainder of Acts 16.) The whole city was thrown into an uproar because a single slave girl was delivered from a spirit of divination.

At that point, Paul was not merely dealing with Satan's kingdom on the natural, physical plane. This was an eruption of Satan's kingdom in the heavenlies because its strategy against the church was being frustrated. It is remarkable to note that almost everywhere Paul went, there was a riot.

Later, in 2 Corinthians, Paul said that an angel of Satan had come to buffet him. (See 2 Corinthians 12:7.) I believe that was not a metaphor. It was just as he said. He battled a satanic angel that incited a riot in every city where Paul went.

Why don't we have riots? Maybe we do not bother Satan enough! I believe that when the church is what it ought to be, there will be a lot more riots. There will also be a lot more revivals. I don't know how many revivals we can have without riots. We have to decide, "Is it worth the price?"

3. SORCERY

The third branch we will examine is the sorcery branch. Frequently, but not exclusively, sorcery operates through physical objects such as potions or charms. Basically, this would include anything that is considered "lucky," such as a horseshoe, a rabbit's foot, or whatever else people might carry to bring them luck. Sorcery also operates through love potions, which are fairly common in certain cultures. A woman would say, "I want this man to fall in love with me, so I'll go to the witch doctor, get a potion, and put it in his food. After that, he'll fall in love with me."

My wife Ruth and I were once in Zambia together with some Christian brothers and sisters. During our time of

I BELIEVE THE TREMENDOUS UPSURGE OF VIOLENCE IN OUR CONTEMPORARY CIVILIZATION IS LARGELY THE WORK OF SORCERY. WHEN WE PRAY ABOUT THESE ISSUES, BEYOND PRAYING FOR THE SYMPTOMS, WE NEED TO DEAL WITH THEIR CORE—SORCERY.

ministry there, we offered a prayer for all the women who were barren—unable to have children. For Africans, this condition is a real disaster. About four hundred professing Christian ladies presented themselves for prayer. Before we prayed, however, we asked the question, "How many of you went to the witch doctor for a potion to deliver you from barrenness?" All but two of them raised their hands! It made us realize we were not dealing with practices that were rare or uncommon.

Sorcery also operates through drugs. The Greek word for *sorcery* is directly formed from the Greek word for "a drug." The entire drug culture is a clear example of sorcery at work. Most people who come to Jesus out of that culture will need to be delivered from the power of sorcery.

Let us look at just one biblical reference to sorcery; it is found in Revelation 9. This passage describes a future scene in human history when God's judgments are being manifested and are falling on the wicked:

> *But the rest of mankind, who were not killed by these plagues, did not repent of the works of their hands, that they should not worship demons, and idols of gold, silver, brass, stone, and wood, which can neither see nor hear nor walk. And they did not repent of their murders or their sorceries or their sexual immorality or their thefts.*
>
> (Revelation 9:20–21)

Sexual immorality and violence go together with sorcery. I believe the tremendous upsurge of violence in our contemporary civilization is largely the work of sorcery. When we pray about these issues, beyond praying for the symptoms, we need to deal with their core—sorcery.

FOURTEEN

HOW WITCHCRAFT OPERATES

"And my speech and my preaching were not with
persuasive words of human wisdom,
but in demonstration of the Spirit and of power."
—1 Corinthians 2:4

We have already seen that witchcraft, expressed as rebellion, produces and supports an illegitimate authority. Rebellion has manifested itself through specific activities in the church that are produced illegally. In this chapter, I will cite examples, as well as the alternatives that are subverted in this process.

THE CARNAL OVER THE SPIRITUAL

Witchcraft promotes the carnal and suppresses the spiritual. In terms of Old Testament patterns, witchcraft puts Ishmael over Isaac. That is precisely what Islam has done.

Islam teaches that Abraham did not sacrifice Isaac but rather Ishmael. Muslims believe that Ishmael is the appointed heir. Putting Ishmael over Isaac is witchcraft. Of course, there are a lot more "Ishmaels" than this one example from Islam. Anything we do by our own initiative, which is not initiated by God through the Holy Spirit, will be an Ishmael.

Jesus never did anything by His own initiative. He said, *"The Son can do nothing of Himself, but what He sees the Father do"* (John 5:19). The moment we try to start something that is not initiated by God, we are going to produce an Ishmael.

Abraham's experience should be a stern warning to us. Four thousand years ago, Abraham produced Ishmael, and for all the ensuing years, the appointed seed of Abraham has had problems with Ishmael. These problems are coming to a climax in the Middle East right now.

THEOLOGY OVER REVELATION

Witchcraft produces its own theology and sets it over divine revelation. This is one of the major problems of the church. I would have to say, frankly, that many seminaries today are producing servants of Satan. That is a shocking, but true, statement.

Most of the problems of the church result from exalting human thinking above divine revelation. This is certainly not true of all seminaries. But, in my opinion, it is true of many seminaries today.

EDUCATION OVER DISCIPLING

Witchcraft in the church exalts education above discipling. If we were to go to a theological seminary or a Bible school and sit in classes for three years, we would get a lot of head knowledge. What does knowledge do? It puffs up.

Jesus didn't do that. He made His disciples follow behind Him and serve Him.

If we do not combine training with serving, we are going to produce the wrong results. The only safeguard against giving people knowledge is to enable them to serve.

PSYCHOLOGY OVER DISCERNMENT

Witchcraft exalts psychology above discernment. In other words, it promotes psychological treatment over a legitimate spiritual word of knowledge.

When Jesus met the woman at the well, He did not ask her about her childhood, when she was born, whether she had problems with her parents, or whether there was a social stigma in her life. He just said, "You have had five husbands." And that was all He needed to say. One word of knowledge eliminates the need for a whole lot of psychology.

PROGRAMS OVER SUPERNATURAL DIRECTION

Witchcraft exalts programs above supernatural direction. The apostles never came up with a program for evangelizing Judea. They were simply sent out by the Holy Spirit. There was no program for sending Philip to Samaria; the Holy Spirit simply brought him there. And the results followed.

ELOQUENCE OVER SUPERNATURAL POWER

Witchcraft exalts eloquence above supernatural power. Jesus never gave His disciples training in homiletics. Charles Finney once said, "All the homiletical training that I've ever seen has had one aim—to make people speak as if they really meant what they were saying." Paul was a very highly educated man, and yet he said:

*And I, brethren, when I came to you, did not come with
excellence of speech or of wisdom declaring to you the testimony of God. For I determined not to know anything
among you except Jesus Christ and Him crucified.*

(1 Corinthians 2:1–2)

In effect, he was saying, "I am not going to let witchcraft
obscure Jesus and the cross." This is significant because just
before he went to Corinth, Paul was in Athens. In Athens, he
tried to meet the people on their own ground. He quoted Greek
poets, and he engaged the Athenians on an intellectual basis,
but the results were very disappointing. I suppose somewhere
between Athens and Corinth, Paul said, "That's the end of that!
From now on, all I am going to do is present Jesus crucified."
And the results in Corinth were tremendous: one of the largest
churches in the early world took root and grew there.

But Paul had to make a decision: *"I determined not to know
anything...except Jesus Christ and Him crucified"* (1 Corinthians
2:2). Without question, witchcraft opposes the revelation of
Jesus crucified.

*I was with you in weakness, in fear, and in much trembling.
And my speech and my preaching were not with persuasive
words of human wisdom, but in demonstration of the Spirit
and of power.* (verses 3–4)

Those are the alternatives: human eloquence or supernatural demonstration.

REASONING OVER FAITH

Witchcraft exalts reasoning above the walk of faith. God
doesn't lead us by reasoning; He leads us step-by-step in a life

WITCHCRAFT EXALTS REASONING ABOVE THE WALK OF FAITH. GOD DOESN'T LEAD US BY REASONING; HE LEADS US STEP-BY-STEP IN A LIFE OF FAITH. HE DOES NOT TELL US THE WHOLE PLAN OF WHERE WE ARE GOING TO GO OR WHAT IS GOING TO HAPPEN. HE SIMPLY SAYS, "THIS IS THE NEXT MOVE."

of faith. As He dealt with Abraham, He deals with us. He does not tell us the whole plan of where we are going to go or what is going to happen. He simply says, "This is the next move."

As we walk in faith, we have the supernatural attestation of the Holy Spirit with us. When we rely on our own reasoning, all we receive is what reason can produce.

LEGALISM OVER LOVE

Finally, witchcraft exalts legalism above love. Doesn't it seem true that most legalistic, religious people are very unloving? Basically, we shy away from them. We don't want them wagging their finger at us and telling us, "Don't do this" and "Don't do that." Such people are very critical of others. Anyone who does not keep their set of rules is wrong.

> *For in Christ Jesus neither circumcision nor uncircumcision avails anything, but faith working through love.*
> (Galatians 5:6)

What really matters most is faith working through love. And notice what kind of faith. It is not a theological faith or a faith that majors on doctrinal hairsplitting. It is a faith that operates through love.

Each of the above tactics is part of Satan's diabolical strategy to obscure Jesus crucified. Once the church loses sight of what was accomplished on the cross, it can no longer administer Jesus's victory over Satan.

Witchcraft has blinded the eyes of the church to this essential, fundamental truth. We must make a determined effort to throw off the veil of witchcraft and fix our gaze on the work of the cross.

FIFTEEN

THE WORK OF THE CROSS

"For the message of the cross is foolishness
to those who are perishing, but to us who are being saved
it is the power of God."
—1 Corinthians 1:18

Let us keep in the forefront of our minds, as we have seen throughout this book, that on the cross, Jesus administered to Satan a total, irrevocable, eternal defeat. Nothing can ever change that. Satan can never recover from that defeat, but Jesus has left it to the church to administer His victory. So, Satan's tactic is to keep the church from advancing by obscuring what happened on the cross. As I stated in previous chapters, the evil force that obscures the work of the cross is called *witchcraft*.

LOSING SIGHT OF THE CROSS

The church today is in a condition similar to that of the Galatian church as described by Paul in a passage we reviewed earlier:

> O foolish Galatians! Who has bewitched you that you should not obey the truth, before whose eyes Jesus Christ was clearly portrayed among you as crucified?
>
> (Galatians 3:1)

Once again, what has witchcraft done? It has obscured Jesus crucified. And, remember, once the church loses sight of what was accomplished on the cross, it can no longer administer Jesus's victory over Satan.

We must be careful to safeguard ourselves, and the safeguards all come through applying the work of the cross in our own lives.

LIVING THE VICTORY

There are two aspects to the work of the cross: (1) what Jesus *did* for us, and (2) what He *will do* in us. First, He provided everything we will ever need, and He defeated our enemy. That is what Jesus did for us. However, many people who get excited about what He did *for* us have never begun to understand what the cross is intended to do *in* us.

If the cross does not have its work *in* us, we will not fully benefit from the victory because our subtle, deceptive enemy will get the better of us and corrupt us.

In the next few chapters, we will focus on the five operations of the cross in the life of the believer. We will see what the cross

THERE ARE TWO ASPECTS TO THE

WORK OF THE CROSS: (1) WHAT

JESUS *DID* FOR US, AND (2) WHAT

HE *WILL DO* IN US. IF THE CROSS

DOES NOT HAVE ITS WORK *IN* US,

WE WILL NOT FULLY BENEFIT FROM

THE VICTORY BECAUSE OUR SUBTLE,

DECEPTIVE ENEMY WILL GET THE

BETTER OF US AND CORRUPT US.

has delivered us from, thereby enabling us to step into the victory God desires for us over our enemy, the devil.

In a sense, this is not popular preaching. I am not going to tell you how to get rich quick, how to solve all your problems, or how to get all your prayers answered in the next six months. I am going to outline for you the vital truth of the victorious work of the cross. Let me preface the material that follows by saying emphatically that Jesus was never more victorious than when He was on the cross.

SIXTEEN

DELIVERANCE #1: THIS PRESENT EVIL AGE

"That He might deliver us from this present evil age."
—Galatians 1:4

W e begin this chapter with Paul's greeting to the Galatians:

Grace to you and peace from God the Father and our Lord Jesus Christ, who gave Himself for our sins, that He might deliver us from this present evil age, according to the will of our God and Father. (Galatians 1:3–4)

Our first point is, I believe, the primary deliverance. Until we understand that it is God's purpose, through the cross, that we be delivered from this present evil age, we are not really aligned with what God intends to do for us and through us.

Four other deliverances through the cross follow in Galatians, and we will look at each of them. But I believe the other four are the outworking of this primary deliverance, which is from this present evil age. Do we fully realize that it is God's purpose to deliver us from this present evil age?

THE PRESENT WORLD ORDER

Two Greek words in the New Testament describing our current society are not always accurately translated, so we need to examine them closely. The first word, *kosmos*—from which we get such words as *cosmology* and *cosmonaut*—is properly translated "world." But as it is used in the New Testament, this word doesn't refer to "the globe." It means "the present world order."

The distinctive feature of the present world order is that it is not submitted to the righteous government of God. It is an order in rebellion against God. In John chapter 15, the word *"world"* occurs five times in one verse. This is what Jesus said to His disciples:

> *If you were of the world, the world would love its own. Yet because you are not of the world, but I chose you out of the world, therefore the world hates you.* (John 15:19)

We see here a total line of separation between the world and the church. The world is in rebellion against God. The church, on the other hand, is a group of people called out from the world. That is what the word *church* means: "a called-out company." We are called out by the sovereign choice of Jesus to become the people of God, submitted to God. The more the church is submitted to God, the more the world will hate it.

Jesus said to His biological brothers, who wanted Him to seek worldly fame, "*The world cannot hate you* [because you belong to it], *but it hates Me because I testify about it, that its deeds are evil*" (John 7:7 NASB). If the world doesn't hate the church

UNTIL WE UNDERSTAND THAT IT
IS GOD'S PURPOSE, THROUGH THE
CROSS, THAT WE BE DELIVERED
FROM THIS PRESENT EVIL AGE,
WE ARE NOT REALLY ALIGNED
WITH WHAT GOD INTENDS TO DO
FOR US AND THROUGH US.

today, it is because the world is permeating the church. Why should the world hate its own?

There is a modern-day teaching that the church is going to take over the world. I don't believe that. At the present moment, it is the other way around. The world has taken over the church. If the world were evicted from the church, and the church were separated from the world, we would discover how much the world really hates the church.

THE PRESENT EVIL AGE

The second Greek word used in the New Testament for modern society is *aion*, which gives us the English word *eon*, meaning "an age." It is a measurement of time.

God's time plan consists of ages that follow one another, and the strongest phrase in the Bible, "*forever and ever,*" means "to the ages of ages."[2] The meaning is "ages, each of which is made up of ages." The human mind can't even begin to comprehend the depth of that phrase.

Let's look again at the way the word "*age*" appears in Galatians: "[Christ] *gave Himself for our sins, that He might deliver us from this present evil age*" (Galatians 1:4).

The Bible reveals certain simple, objective facts about this present age. First of all, the most important fact is that it is coming to an end. It is not going to last forever. All of us might say, "Thank God!" for that. Personally, I do not want the present age to continue. I think it is a mess, and it is getting steadily worse.

2. See 1 Chronicles 29:10; Nehemiah 9:5; Psalm 9:5; 10:16; 21:4; 45:6, 17; 48:14; 52:8; 111:8; 119:44; 145:1–2, 21; 148:6; Isaiah 30:8; 45:17; Jeremiah 7:7; 25:5; Daniel 2:20; 12:3; Micah 4:5; Galatians 1:5; Ephesians 3:21; Philippians 4:20; 1 Timothy 1:17; 2 Timothy 4:18; Hebrews 1:8; 13:21; 1 Peter 4:11; 5:11; Revelation 1:6; 4:9–10; 5:13–14; 7:12; 10:6; 11:15; 14:11; 15:7; 19:3; 20:10; 22:5.

"Age" also appears in Matthew 13. In this great parable of the kingdom, Jesus is interpreting the significance of the wheat and the tares.

> *The enemy who sowed them [the tares] is the devil, the harvest is the end of the age, and the reapers are the angels.*
>
> (Matthew 13:39)

Jesus said the harvest is the end of the age. The following verses reveal that when the harvest comes, the age is going to end.

> *Therefore as the tares are gathered and burned in the fire, so it will be at the end of this age. The Son of Man will send out His angels, and they will gather out of His kingdom all things that offend, and those who practice lawlessness, and will cast them into the furnace of fire. There will be wailing and gnashing of teeth. Then the righteous will shine forth as the sun in the kingdom of their Father. He who has ears to hear, let him hear!* (Matthew 13:40–43)

The righteous and the wicked are going to coexist right up to the end of the age. We need to keep in mind that it is not our business to separate them. It is too difficult.

In the parable, the workers said, "Shall we go and pull up the tares?" and the landowner said, "No, because you might pull up some of the wheat with them." (See Matthew 13:28–29.) But Jesus said, "At the end of the age, I'll send out My angels. They'll pull out the tares, and the wheat will be left."

In the same chapter, in the parable of the dragnet, Jesus said:

> *Again, the kingdom of heaven is like a dragnet that was cast into the sea and gathered some of every kind, which,*

when it was full, they drew to shore; and they sat down and gathered the good into vessels, but threw the bad away. So it will be at the end of the age. The angels will come forth, separate the wicked from among the just, and cast them into the furnace of fire. (Matthew 13:47–50)

It is extremely important for us to realize that this age is coming to an end. If we live as if it were to go on forever, we will be living in a delusion.

THE GOD OF THIS AGE

The next fact about this age states the reason why it is an evil age.

But even if our gospel is veiled, it is veiled to those who are perishing, whose minds the god of this age has blinded.
(2 Corinthians 4:3–4)

Who blinds the minds of unbelievers? Satan. And what is he? He is *"the god of this age."* No wonder he does not want the age to end. Because when this age ends, he will no longer be a god. But the church's responsibility is to bring the age to an end, thereby terminating the rule of Satan as a god.

In the sixth chapter of Hebrews, the writer speaks of those people who had deep spiritual experiences tasting the powers of a new age. But those same people had later fallen away from what they had experienced.

For it is impossible for those who were once enlightened, and have tasted the heavenly gift, and have become partakers of the Holy Spirit, and have tasted the good word of God and the powers of the age to come, if they fall away, to renew

SATAN IS *"THE GOD OF THIS AGE."*

NO WONDER HE DOES NOT WANT

THE AGE TO END. BECAUSE WHEN

THIS AGE ENDS, HE WILL NO LONGER

BE A GOD. BUT THE CHURCH'S

RESPONSIBILITY IS TO BRING THE AGE

TO AN END, THEREBY TERMINATING

THE RULE OF SATAN AS A GOD.

them again to repentance, since they crucify again for them-
selves the Son of God, and put Him to an open shame.

(Hebrews 6:4–6)

Five experiences are specified here. We have been enlightened, we have tasted the heavenly gift (eternal life), we have
become partakers of the Holy Spirit, we have tasted the good
Word of God, and we have savored the powers of the age to
come.

To me, this is what comes with the baptism in the Holy
Spirit. When you are baptized in the Spirit, you are immersed
in a supernatural presence. It is supernatural in this age and will
be natural in the next age. In this age, we have been given a little
taste of what the power of the next age will be like. God has
given us a taste in order to spoil our taste for this age. Why
should Christians be enamored of the tastes of this age when we
have tasted the powers of the age to come?

RESISTING THIS AGE

Now he who received seed among the thorns is he who hears
the word, and the cares of this world and the deceitfulness of
riches choke the word, and he becomes unfruitful.

(Matthew 13:22)

Where it says *"world"* in the *New King James Version*, the
correct translation is *"age"* (as in Young's Literal Translation).
The worries of this age choke the Word of God in our lives and
make us unfruitful. We cannot afford to be part of "this age,"
because, if we are, we will be dominated by its cares and its
problems. They will make us spiritually unfruitful. We have to
live lives that belong to a different age.

And do not be conformed to this world [the correct translation is "do not be conformed to this age"], *but be transformed by the renewing of your mind, that you may prove what is that good and acceptable and perfect will of God.*

(Romans 12:2)

We cannot afford to be conformed to the present age. Our solution is not a list of religious rules, because that does not change people on the inside. The solution is for our minds to be changed, because when we begin to think differently, we will live differently. That is the difference between religion and grace.

Religion consists of outside rules—what types of clothing we should wear, what length our hair must be, how much makeup we may use, and other external observances. Paul is essentially saying, "Do not think the way this age thinks. Be changed in your mind. Let the Holy Spirit give you a different way of thinking and evaluating things, different priorities, different ambitions, different goals. Then you will live differently."

RENEWED MINDS

Then Paul explains that when our minds are renewed, we will discover the good, acceptable, and perfect will of God. Many Christians do not find the will of God because they are never renewed in their minds. The unrenewed mind cannot discover the will of God. As Paul wrote earlier in Romans, *"The carnal mind is enmity against God"* (Romans 8:7). God does not reveal His secrets to His enemies. But if our minds are changed, then God will begin to show us His secrets, including His plan for our lives. I am afraid that millions of Christians who get to heaven will have missed God's plan for them here on earth because they were not renewed in their minds. That is why we are not to be conformed to this present age.

The second book of Timothy tells of one of the great tragedies of the New Testament. One of Paul's most trusted, long-term fellow workers abandoned him. *"Demas has forsaken me, having loved this present world* [age]*"* (2 Timothy 4:10).

This verse does not say that Demas went into sin, that he became immoral or a drunkard. He just was enamored of this present age. He reached a point where the love of this age made it impossible for him to go any further with Paul.

I think that has been true in the experience of many people called to serve the Lord. The love of this age has kept them from fulfilling their calls. A servant of God cannot love this present age. We have to make up our minds to resist the present age.

TWO DISTINCT RESULTS

There are two distinct results of being delivered from this present evil age.

1. CITIZENSHIP IN HEAVEN

Brethren, join in following my example, and note those who so walk, as you have us for a pattern. For many walk, of whom I have told you often, and now tell you even weeping, that they are the enemies of the cross of Christ.

(Philippians 3:17–18)

Notice that those who are described in this passage are not the enemies of Christ but of the cross. In other words, as long as they can get what they want from Jesus, they will be friends with Him.

Whose end is destruction, whose god is their belly, and whose glory is in their shame—who set their mind on earthly things.   (verse 19)

Paul outlines the result of refusing to embrace the cross. We can say nice things about Jesus Christ and call Him our Savior, but if we do not embrace His cross, this will be our destination. For many modern Christians, their god is their belly. To tell the truth, they are more interested in what they put in their stomachs than what they can do for God. No race, ethnicity, or nationality is exempt from that problem.

Yet for those who resist this temptation, Paul says, *"Our citizenship is in heaven"* (Philippians 3:20).

Citizenship in heaven? What does that mean for us? I am privileged to have both British citizenship and American citizenship. But the most important citizenship I have is citizenship in heaven. That is the only one that really matters. That citizenship is the result of embracing the cross and being separated from this present evil age. If you are a Christian, then your citizenship is in heaven.

If you have citizenship in any nation, you are entitled to the passport of that country. When you come to the nation where you are a citizen, you are admitted on very different terms than people who do not have that passport.

Have you ever stood in the immigration line at an airport and watched how people are received? My wife is only an American citizen, so when I go to Britain with her, I go in with my American passport. We stand in the line that says, "Other Passports." Everyone with a UK passport just walks right through. But when we return to the United States, then it is the other people who have to wait, while we walk right through. It is important to have the right passport. And you can only have the right passport if you have the right citizenship. You need citizenship in heaven to have heaven's passport—the right of free entry into the country of which you are a citizen.

2. LOOKING FOR CHRIST'S RETURN

Not only do we have citizenship in heaven, but we also look for Christ's return to earth. That is the second mark of being delivered from this present evil age. Paul expresses it this way:

> For our citizenship is in heaven, from which we also eagerly wait for the Savior, the Lord Jesus Christ.
> (Philippians 3:20)

Are we eagerly waiting for the Lord Jesus Christ? He is only coming back for the people who are eagerly waiting for Him.

> And as it is appointed for men to die once, but after this the judgment, so Christ was offered once to bear the sins of many. To those who eagerly wait for Him He will appear a second time, apart from sin, for salvation.
> (Hebrews 9:27–28)

He will appear to those who eagerly wait for Him. If we have not been delivered from this present evil age, we will not be eagerly waiting for Jesus. So, the practical results of being delivered from this present evil age through faith in Jesus are that we have citizenship in heaven and we are eagerly awaiting the return of the Lord from heaven.

SEVENTEEN

DELIVERANCE #2: THE LAW

"I through the law am dead to the law."
—Galatians 2:19 (KJV, KJVER)

We turn now to the second deliverance provided by the cross, as described in Galatians. As I said earlier, these remaining four deliverances are various aspects of the primary deliverance: "from this present evil age." This means that to be fully delivered from this present evil age, we need to make sure we have all four subsequent deliverances as well.

THE ONLY WAY OUT

For I through the law died to the law that I might live to God. (Galatians 2:19)

When Christ died, I died to the law. My old man was crucified with Him. So, through the cross and the death of

Jesus—which has become my death through my faith—I have died to the law. That is a wonderful thought, if we can grasp it.

The final thing the law can do to us is put us to death. That is its ultimate penalty. Once it has put us to death, it can do nothing more to us. If a person is executed, he is no longer subject to the law. The only way out from under the law is death.

In the mercy of God, our death took place when Jesus died on the cross. *"I through the law am dead to the law"* (Galatians 2:19 KJV, KJVER). The law has nothing to say to me; I have no more relationship to it. I have been separated from the law by the death of Jesus.

When I would speak to people on this theme, I often saw a look of polite astonishment come on their faces. They simply could not conceive that God's purpose is that we should be delivered from the law. But that is the truth. It is His purpose.

This truth is clearly stated in the Bible many times. Here is one breathtaking statement:

> *For sin shall not have dominion over you, for you are not under law but under grace.* (Romans 6:14)

Previously in this book, I referred to two mutually exclusive alternatives: the law and grace. We cannot have them both; we have to make a choice. If we are under law, we are not under grace. If we are under grace, we are not under law. So, we have to make up our minds: "Am I under law or am I under grace?" We cannot have one foot in two different worlds.

THE ONLY WAY OUT FROM UNDER

THE LAW IS DEATH. IN THE MERCY

OF GOD, OUR DEATH TOOK PLACE

WHEN JESUS DIED ON THE CROSS.

THE LAW HAS NOTHING TO

SAY TO US; WE HAVE NO MORE

RELATIONSHIP TO IT. WE HAVE

BEEN SEPARATED FROM THE LAW

BY THE DEATH OF JESUS.

ESCAPING FROM THE LAW

The implication of this truth is that if we are under the law, sin will have dominion over us. What is the obvious conclusion? The only way to escape the dominion of sin is to escape from the law. This option was provided by the death of Jesus on the cross. *"I through the law am dead to the law"* (Galatians 2:19 KJV, KJVER).

> *For when we were in the flesh, the sinful passions which were aroused by the law were at work in our members to bear fruit to death. But now we have been delivered from the law, having died to what we were held by, so that we should serve in the newness of the Spirit and not in the oldness of the letter.* (Romans 7:5–6)

Paul is not talking here about being delivered from sin but about being delivered from the law.

In this complicated passage in Romans 7, Paul uses the analogy of a woman married to a man, and he says, "According to the law, if that woman marries another man while her husband remains alive, she is an adulteress. But once her husband is dead, she's free to marry another man." (See verse 3.)

According to Paul, we had been under the law, married to our carnal nature. Out of that union, the carnal nature produced what it always produces—the works of the flesh. Not one good work among them. But Paul conveys the good news that, on the cross, our carnal nature died in Jesus. Now, we are free to "marry another" without being an adulteress. To whom shall we be married? Christ. If we are married to the resurrected Christ, our union with Him will bring forth the fruit of the Spirit. (See Galatians 5:22–23.)

FLESH OR SPIRIT?

There are two possible unions. You can be united with your fleshly nature and bring forth the works of the flesh—marriage under the law. Or, you can be delivered from the law, free to be united to Jesus by the Holy Spirit in a marriage relationship and bring forth the fruit of the Spirit.

In neither case is it a question of trying or doing our best. Christianity is not a religion of effort or a religion of doing our best. The key word is *union*. We bring forth what is appropriate to what we unite with.

United to our fleshly nature, no matter how hard we try or how many rules we make, we will only bring forth the works of the flesh—again, not one good work among them. On the other hand, when we are truly united to Jesus the resurrected Lord by the Holy Spirit, we will naturally bring forth the fruit of the Spirit—without human effort.

It is therefore not effort but union. It is not a new set of rules but relationship. This principle is so plainly stated in the New Testament that it is amazing the majority of professing Christians have never known it.

Another very simple picture of spiritual union with Christ is the parable of the vine, which is found in John 15. Jesus said, *"I am the vine, you are the branches. He who abides in Me, and I in him, bears much fruit"* (John 15:5). Jesus also said, *"I am the true vine, and My Father is the vinedresser"* (verse 1). This is a beautiful parable of the Godhead and what happens when we abide in the Lord. Where is the Holy Spirit in this picture? He is the sap. The branches do not produce fruit by trying hard but by abiding in the vine. When they abide in the vine, they cannot help but produce fruit. It is not effort but union.

We see, therefore, that we have been delivered from the law to bring an end to the fleshly activity it produced within us. As Paul says, *"Those who are in the flesh cannot please God"* (Romans 8:8). On the positive side, we are delivered from the law to be united with Jesus, producing fruit pleasing to God.

THREE FREEDOMS

Let us now examine three key results of being delivered from the law.

1. FREEDOM FROM CONDEMNATION

First of all, we receive freedom from condemnation.

There is therefore now no condemnation to those who are in Christ Jesus.... For what the law could not do in that it was weak through the flesh, God did by sending His own Son in the likeness of sinful flesh. (Romans 8:1, 3)

The book of Romans is like percolated coffee. Percolated coffee takes longer to make than instant coffee because it has to go through the brewing process.

We cannot get instant coffee out of Romans 8. We must go through the preceding seven chapters. That is the percolator. But the result is so much richer. Only when we have been through those chapters do we get to the *"therefore."*

The preceding chapters in Romans deal with the total sinfulness of all humanity and with the failure of religion to change man's sinful nature. Using the examples of Abraham and David

WHEN WE ARE TRULY UNITED TO

JESUS THE RESURRECTED LORD

BY THE HOLY SPIRIT, WE WILL

NATURALLY BRING FORTH THE

FRUIT OF THE SPIRIT—WITHOUT

HUMAN EFFORT.

(chapter 4), with a comparison between Adam and Christ (chapter 5), chapter 6 then reveals God's remedy for the old man: execution. God doesn't patch him up. He doesn't reform him. He doesn't send him to church. He executes him! The good news is that this execution took place when Jesus died on the cross.

Romans 7 deals with our relationship to the law. I always used to think, "Why come to the law after all that?" But I have learned by my own experience, by dealing with people, and by the teaching of Scripture, that the ultimate hurdle we have to get over (the last stage of this percolator) is how we relate to the law.

Most Christians have never gotten over that hurdle. Without the percolator, we cannot live in Romans 8, because the essential condition is *"no condemnation."* The moment we come under condemnation, we are out of the Spirit-controlled life of Romans 8. The devil's number one objective is to bring us under condemnation. The purpose of God's Word, especially in Romans, is to deliver us from condemnation.

2. FREEDOM TO LOVE

Second, deliverance from the law brings a freedom to love. Just as the law and grace are opposed to each other, so are legalism and love. As I expressed earlier, in a legalistic system, it is very hard to love.

> *Owe no one anything except to love one another, for he who loves another has fulfilled the law.*   (Romans 13:8)

Notice that the person who loves *"has fulfilled the law."* It is not something they still have to accomplish.

For the commandments, "You shall not commit adultery,"
"You shall not murder," "You shall not steal," "You shall
not bear false witness," "You shall not covet," and if there is
any other commandment, are all summed up in this saying,
namely, "You shall love your neighbor as yourself." Love
does no harm to a neighbor; therefore love is the fulfillment
of the law.   (Romans 13:9–10)

That last statement is very simple. In fact, the problem for theologians is that this principle seems too simple. Yet it is true. Galatians adds this insight, which we previously noted:

For in Christ Jesus neither circumcision nor uncircumcision
avails anything, but faith working through love.
                                          (Galatians 5:6)

In the last resort, what matters most is faith working through love. If we ever get away from that truth, we have become sidetracked. We can get focused on all sorts of theological theories, interpretations, and beliefs. But if we ever stray away from faith working through love, we have gone off-center. We have missed the central purpose of the gospel message.

For all the law is fulfilled in one word, even in this: "You
shall love your neighbor as yourself."   (Galatians 5:14)

Such love is not possible when the law binds us, because we are bound to our carnal nature. As we have seen, what the carnal nature produces is anything but good fruit.

3. FREEDOM TO BE LED BY THE HOLY SPIRIT

The third result of being delivered from the law is freedom to be led by the Holy Spirit.

For as many as are led by the Spirit of God, these are sons of God. For you did not receive the spirit of bondage [slavery] again to fear, but you received the Spirit of adoption by whom we cry out, "Abba, Father."   (Romans 8:14–15)

As I have stated before, God has not given us the spirit of slavery but the spirit of "sonship." God does not want to produce slaves. He wants to produce sons and daughters. The defining mark of sons and daughters of God is stated here very clearly: *"For as many as are [regularly] led by the Spirit of God, these are sons of God."*

Most people with a Pentecostal or charismatic church background have heard sermons on how to be born again, and probably how to be baptized in the Holy Spirit. Both are tremendous truths. The new birth makes us children of God. The baptism in the Holy Spirit equips us to serve God with supernatural power. But the only way we can become mature sons and daughters of God is by being led by the Holy Spirit.

I have spoken before large congregations and asked, "How many of you have ever heard a sermon on how to be led by the Holy Spirit?" Very often, not more than 25 percent will raise their hands, which indicates a great deficiency. We place all our focus on the onetime experiences and do not realize the importance of the ongoing life in the Spirit.

The words in Romans 8:14 are in the continuing present. This verse says, in essence, "As many as are being regularly led by the Spirit of God, they (and only they) are sons of God." Put this together with Galatians 5:18 to see the full effect of what I am trying to share: *"But if you are led by the Spirit, you are not under the law."*

DELIVERANCE FROM THE LAW

MEANS A RELEASE TO BECOME

A MATURE SON OR DAUGHTER OF

GOD THROUGH BEING LED BY THE

HOLY SPIRIT.

If we want to be led by the Spirit, we cannot be under the law. And if we are not led by the Spirit, we cannot become mature sons and daughters of God. Deliverance from the law means a release to become a mature son or daughter of God through being led by the Holy Spirit.

I want to emphasize this point: the Holy Spirit is a person. He is not a set of rules, nor is He a theological concept. He is not half a sentence at the end of the Apostle's Creed; He is a person. We have to learn to relate to Him as a person and be sensitive to Him.

I realize this is a tremendous problem for religious people. They think, "If I let go of the rules, what will I hold on to? This is dangerous." Ironically, the Bible tells us what is truly dangerous: to try to live by the rules.

There is definitely a place for rules. I believe in being an obedient citizen of the nation in which I live. For example, I believe in observing the speed limit. I also believe there need to be simple, practical rules for a family. I believe in a few simple principles to guide the conduct of the affairs of the church. But we are not made righteous by keeping the rules.

If we have been made righteous by faith, and the rules are right, we will keep them. But our righteousness does not come from keeping those rules. If the only righteousness we have is by keeping rules (which is true of millions of Christians), we will never experience the righteousness God intends us to have.

EIGHTEEN

DELIVERANCE #3: SELF

*"I have been crucified with Christ; it is no longer
I who live, but Christ lives in me; and the life which I now
live in the flesh I live by faith in the Son of God,
who loved me and gave Himself for me."*
—Galatians 2:20

It is appropriate that deliverance from self is the central deliverance out of the five. I do not believe we can ever find the fullness of God's will for our lives or enjoy the full provision of the cross until we allow the cross to put *self* to death.

A ROOT OF EVIL

Self is the root of many evils that are common in the church: pride, egotism, personal ambition, and sectarianism. All these represent the uncrucified ego. Racism is another aspect of the uncrucified ego, and we see much racism, even in the Christian church.

When I was pastoring in England in the 1950s, we had a dear "spiritual sister" in our congregation who prayed like an angel for the people of Africa. But when a black brother would sit down next to her, it really disturbed her. There is a lot of undercover racism left in us, and it is very contrary to the purposes of God for the church.

> *Let nothing be done through selfish ambition or conceit, but in lowliness of mind let each esteem others better than himself.* (Philippians 2:3)

The attitude described here is a result of the crucifixion of the ego. Having such an attitude is impossible until we have let our egos die on the cross. Two traits that mark the church very conspicuously are competitiveness and personal ambition. As a minister, I have seen a tremendous amount of personal ambition and competitiveness in Christian ministry today. The cause? Our egos have not been dealt with on the cross.

ETHICAL BLEMISHES

I will now point out the real dividing line between the true church and the world today. In 2 Timothy, Paul gives us a very striking description of the degeneration of human character that will mark the close of this age. How many of these eighteen moral and ethical blemishes are conspicuous in our current society?

> *But know this, that in the last days perilous times will come: for men will be lovers of themselves, lovers of money, boasters,*

SELF IS THE ROOT OF MANY EVILS

THAT ARE COMMON IN THE CHURCH:

PRIDE, EGOTISM,

PERSONAL AMBITION,

SECTARIANISM, AND RACISM.

*proud, blasphemers, disobedient to parents, unthank-
ful, unholy, unloving, unforgiving, slanderers, without
self-control, brutal, despisers of good, traitors, headstrong,
haughty, lovers of pleasures rather than lovers of God.*

(2 Timothy 3:1–4)

You might say, "This is a terrible list, but at least we don't
find these blemishes in the church." That is a huge mistake,
because the next verse says,

...having a form of godliness....   (2 Timothy 3:5)

I do not believe Paul would ever have used the word *godliness*
in relation to a religion that had nothing to do with the Bible or
with Jesus Christ. These are people who have made some kind
of profession of church membership. But Paul goes on to say:

...but denying its power.   (verse 5)

These who deny the power of godliness to radically change
human nature are religious, but they just go on living the same
kind of life they lived before they professed religion.

The list above begins and ends with what people love. The
first item in the list is *"lovers of themselves,"* the next is *"lovers of
money,"* and the last is *"lovers of pleasures."*

THREE "LOVES"

Let's consider those three characteristics for a moment—
love of self, love of money, and love of pleasure. They are probably the three most characteristic features of our contemporary
culture. I would quickly add that the root of all is the first one—
love of self.

The mere fact that people do not swear, gamble, or abuse alcohol, tobacco, or drugs does not necessarily indicate that they are Christians. We cannot base our claim to being a Christian on the fact that we do not do these obvious sins because, for example, we might still be very selfish.

The real distinguishing line between the world and the true church is whether people are lovers of self or whether self has been crucified, and they are living for something other than themselves.

We often hear this parody of the typical prayer of the average church member: "God bless me and my wife; my son, John; and his wife—us four, no more. Amen." That sounds religious, but it is actually extremely selfish, isn't it? How many of us are self-centered in our prayers? How many of us ever pray beyond a little narrow circle of the matters that interest *us* and concern *us*?

Thankfully, God has provided a way of release from this focus. It comes through the cross. We can make this decision and affirmation: *"I have been crucified with Christ; it is no longer I who live, but Christ lives in me"* (Galatians 2:20).

That step requires two actions: first of all, a decision, and, second, the right confession. It is important to make a personal confession. In Romans 6, Paul says, *"Our old man was crucified with Him"* (verse 6). That is a general statement. But in Galatians 2:20, Paul makes it his personal testimony: *"I have been crucified with Christ; it is no longer I who live, but Christ lives in me."*

THE CRUCIFIED EGO

There are three direct results of the crucified ego in our lives.

1. FREEDOM TO SERVE

First of all, there is the freedom to serve.

Jesus called them [His disciples] to Himself and said to them, "You know that those who are considered rulers over the Gentiles lord it over them, and their great ones exercise authority over them. Yet it shall not be so among you; but whoever desires to become great among you shall be your servant. And whoever of you desires to be first shall be slave of all."   (Mark 10:42–44)

Several years ago, a young man came to me who was a committed Christian, a man with considerable gifts. He said to me, "Brother Prince, I want to serve you." Well, that wasn't altogether good news to me, because I am a very self-sufficient person. I thought, "I'm really getting along all right without you. If you start serving me, I'm going to have you on the scene at a lot of times when I'd rather be on my own. And you're going to be observing me in situations when I might not wish to be observed." So, I said, "I'll think it over." But when I prayed, the Lord said, "If you don't give that young man an opportunity to serve you, you shut the only door to his legitimate promotion." I told the young man, "Okay." We built a wonderful relationship, and God steadily promoted him in the kingdom. What a great lesson that was for me.

Promotion does not come from man; it comes from God. Jesus said that if we want to be great, we have to become servants. If we want to be the master, we have to become the slave. (See, for example, Matthew 20:26.) In other words, the higher up you want to go, the lower down you have to start. Once again, consider the words of Jesus in Matthew 23:12 and Luke 14:11:

THE REAL DISTINGUISHING LINE

BETWEEN THE WORLD AND THE TRUE

CHURCH IS WHETHER PEOPLE ARE

LOVERS OF SELF OR WHETHER SELF

HAS BEEN CRUCIFIED. WE CAN MAKE

THIS DECISION AND AFFIRMATION:

"I HAVE BEEN CRUCIFIED WITH CHRIST;

IT IS NO LONGER I WHO LIVE, BUT

CHRIST LIVES IN ME" (GALATIANS 2:20).

"Whoever exalts himself will be humbled, and he who humbles himself will be exalted." That is a rule that governs the universe. Do you want promotion? I can guarantee it to you. Just humble yourself and submit to a low place. Find somewhere or someone to serve. But you will not be able to do that as long as the ego in you has not been dealt with. The uncrucified ego corrupts service.

The path to authority and leadership in the church is through serving. There is no other legitimate way. Anyone who comes to a position of authority in the church by any other path will not be able to exercise authority rightly.

2. FREEDOM FROM SELF-EFFORT

The second result of the crucified ego is freedom from self-effort and self-promotion. What a glorious deliverance!

For we do not preach ourselves, but Christ Jesus the Lord, and ourselves your bondservants ["slaves" in Greek] *for Jesus' sake.*   (2 Corinthians 4:5)

That would be a remarkable statement at any time, but when we consider who made it and to whom, it is much more remarkable. Consider the very self-righteous Pharisee, Saul of Tarsus, who had been brought up to believe that he and his nation were the only chosen ones. Saul had been taught to live a certain kind of very strict life and observe a whole list of regulations. Otherwise, he would be impure and unclean. As a Jew, Saul even would have referred to Gentiles as "dogs." Then he met Jesus on the Damascus road, and Jesus changed him!

Some years later, we find Saul, now named Paul, writing to the believers in Corinth, a wicked seaport. The list of what these people had been doing is somewhat shocking. They were prostitutes, pimps, homosexuals, drunkards; every kind of vile sin had been practiced among them. But they had been gloriously changed by the power of the gospel! (See 1 Corinthians 6:9–11.)

Let's consider what it meant for Paul to write to those people and say, "We're not preaching ourselves, but we're preaching Jesus Christ the Lord, and ourselves as your slaves for Jesus's sake." That is the crucified ego!

In 1957, I went to Kenya in East Africa for five years to train African teachers for African schools. I do not consider myself a racially prejudiced person. After all, by that time, I had eight adopted daughters of whom six were Jewish, one was Arab, and one was English. But, when I came to that situation, and I really wanted God to have His way, I had to decide for myself who I really was.

I was a graduate of Cambridge. I was a scholar of Eton. From the point of view of the academic life of Britain, I had reached the pinnacle. All of my ancestors had been officers in the British Army. I really had to ask myself, "Am I willing to say to these black students, 'Not me, but Jesus Christ the Lord; and I'm your servant'?" Thankfully, I can say, to the glory of God, I did it joyfully. And I was never happier in ministry than I was in East Africa.

3. FREEDOM FROM JUSTIFYING OURSELVES

The last result of crucifying the ego is that I do not need to prove myself right. Oh, what a relief! What a blessing! People can disagree with me and argue with me. But I can say, "Let's wait and see who's right. I could be wrong." That is amazing, isn't it? A preacher could be wrong! What a burden was lifted from me when I discovered I didn't have to justify myself. And you can experience the same freedom as you fully surrender your ego to the Lord Jesus Christ.

Thus, the three direct results of the crucified ego in our lives are freedom to serve, freedom from self-effort, and freedom from justifying ourselves. This is the marvelous freedom provided by the cross.

NINETEEN

DELIVERANCE #4: THE FLESH

*"And those who are Christ's have crucified the flesh
with its passions and desires."*
—Galatians 5:24

The fourth deliverance we receive through the cross is freedom from the flesh. The proof that we belong to Jesus Christ is that we have crucified the flesh. That is the evidence. *"Those who are Christ's have crucified the flesh."*

WHAT JESUS SEEKS

In 1 Corinthians 15:23, Paul tells us that when Jesus comes back to the earth, He is coming back for those who are His. The above verse in Galatians tells us that those who are His are those who *"have crucified the flesh with its passions and desires."*

Again, who is Jesus coming back for? Those who have crucified the flesh. He is not coming back for everybody who professes to be a Christian but leads a carnal, selfish, self-indulgent
life. He is coming back for those who have allowed the cross to
do its work in their carnal nature.

> *For the flesh lusts against the Spirit, and the Spirit against
> the flesh; and these are contrary to one another, so that you
> do not do the things that you wish.*   (Galatians 5:17)

Before God changes our fleshly nature, it is in total opposi-
tion to the Spirit of God.

> *So then, those who are in the flesh cannot please God.*
>   (Romans 8:8)

Those who are living according to their old carnal, unregenerate nature cannot please God. Whether they are religious or
unreligious is not important.

OUR RESPONSIBILITY

> *Therefore, brethren, we are debtors—not to the flesh, to live
> according to the flesh. For if you live according to the flesh
> you will die; but if by the Spirit you put to death the deeds of
> the body, you will live.*   (Romans 8:12–13)

It is our responsibility, by the Spirit, to put to death the
deeds of the flesh. Christ has made it possible, but we have to
apply it.

Consider for a moment what is covered by the term "flesh."
It is not just immorality, as some might assume. In fact, that
is not really the main expression of the flesh. Fear, resentment,

JESUS IS NOT COMING BACK FOR
EVERYBODY WHO PROFESSES TO
BE A CHRISTIAN BUT LEADS A
CARNAL, SELFISH,
SELF-INDULGENT LIFE.
HE IS COMING BACK FOR THOSE
WHO HAVE ALLOWED
THE CROSS TO DO ITS WORK IN
THEIR CARNAL NATURE.

anger, greed, covetousness, sexual lusts, and fluctuating moods are all common manifestations of the fleshly nature.

Let us look at moodiness as an example. A moody Christian, first of all, reflects a denial of the faith. The person perhaps lacks trust in God or resists the Spirit's work in their lives. Second, he or she is evidence that the flesh has not been crucified. By the grace of God, I can say I am not a moody person today, because I have allowed the cross to do its work in me and deal with my moods.

We must understand that the flesh wars against the Spirit, and the Spirit against the flesh, in our lives. What is the solution? Deliverance through putting to death the deeds of the flesh and yielding to the Spirit's control of all aspects of our lives.

TWENTY

DELIVERANCE #5: THE WORLD

*"But God forbid that I should boast except in the cross of
our Lord Jesus Christ, by whom [or by which] the world
has been crucified to me, and I to the world."*
—Galatians 6:14

The cross separates us and releases us from a society that is
not subject to the righteous government of God. Jesus said, "You
aren't in the world, because I have called you out of the world."
(See, for example, John 15:19.) This does not mean that God
asks us to close our eyes and ears and walk around as though the
physical, material world does not exist.

There is one simple way to be separated from the world.
It is to be totally committed to the government of Jesus in our
lives.

COMPLETE SEPARATION

As redeemed believers, when we look at the world, between the world and us is a corpse hanging on a cross. When the world looks at us, it sees the same thing. There is a complete separation. It is not a physical separation, but it is in the spiritual realm.

We belong to a totally different realm. We are released from the world's opinions, values, judgments, pressures, enticements, and deceptions—the present world order that is controlled by Satan.

The whole world lies under the sway of the wicked one.
(1 John 5:19)

The great dragon...that serpent of old, called the Devil and Satan, who deceives the whole world.... (Revelation 12:9)

Once Christians begin to come under the influence of the world, they come under deception, because the Spirit of God and the spirit of this world are opposites.

RESULTS OF DELIVERANCE FROM THE WORLD

Now we have received, not the spirit of the world, but the Spirit who is from God, that we might know the things that have been freely given to us by God. (1 Corinthians 2:12)

The spirit of this world will obscure all that has been given to us by God. The Spirit of God will reveal all that He has given us.

There are three results of being delivered from the world.

THE SPIRIT OF THIS WORLD WILL

OBSCURE ALL THAT HAS BEEN

GIVEN TO US BY GOD. THE SPIRIT

OF GOD WILL REVEAL ALL THAT

HE HAS GIVEN US.

1. COMMITMENT TO CHRIST'S KINGDOM

The first result is a commitment to Christ's kingdom.

But seek first the kingdom of God and His righteousness, and all these things shall be added to you. (Matthew 6:33)

I have not been as totally faithful to God as I would have wished. But, looking back, I would have to say I have proved the above Scripture to be effective in my own experience over many years. It is true. It works.

2. FREEDOM FROM SATAN'S MANIPULATION

Second, we are free from Satan's manipulations and deceptions. This is true, especially today, in regard to the effects of the media on us. Such freedom is tremendously important because our minds are continuously being bombarded with various presentations, most of which are false. In the largest sense, they are spiritually untrue.

3. FREEDOM TO REFUSE TO BOW

Finally, release from the dominion of this world means that we will have the power—like Shadrach, Meshach, and Abednego—to refuse to bow before the world's idols. The pressure to bow before the world's idols is tremendous today, especially among young people. These idols include worldly success, popularity, wealth, power, pleasure, and comfort.

Some solemn words in the book of Hebrews will both encourage and challenge us:

So do not throw away your confidence; it will be richly rewarded. You need to persevere so that when you have

done the will of God, you will receive what He has prom-
ised. For, "In just a little while, He who is coming will come
and will not delay." And, "But My righteous one will live
by faith. And I take no pleasure in the one that shrinks
back." But we do not belong to those who shrink back and
are destroyed, but to those who have faith and are saved.
(Hebrews 10:35–39 NIV)

THREE ADMONITIONS

I see three main warnings in the above passage. First, we must not throw away our confidence. For those of us who have strong faith, we must be careful not to give up the good we have received from God.

Second, we need perseverance to obtain the promises of God. It is one thing to fulfill the conditions; it is another to receive the promises. Almost all of us know from experience that there is often a considerable interval of time between our doing what entitles us to the promise and our receiving the fulfillment of the promise. In that interval, we have to practice perseverance.

Third, we must remember the reward is ahead. It is when *"He who is coming will come"* (Hebrews 10:37). That is when the final reward comes. We have to persevere until then. This passage really leaves us with only two alternatives: either we persevere or we shrink back. If we persevere, we will inherit the promise. But if we shrink back, we will be *"destroyed"* (Hebrews 10:39 NIV). This is very strong language. But I am grateful for the honesty of the Word of God that confronts us so frankly.

Which are we going to do? Are we going to persevere? Or are we going to shrink back?

OUR CALL TO BATTLE

You and I are in a battle against an invisible enemy from an invisible kingdom that will use witchcraft in an attempt to destroy mankind—the image of God. Through pride and guilt, Satan attempts to subvert what God has created.

Thankfully, God was willing to stoop down and redeem creation through the one-time sacrifice of His Son, Jesus Christ. Through His death, Jesus disarmed Satan's principalities and powers and forever extinguished the guilt and sin that separated us from God.

NO MORE DOMINATION

Paul says that sin will no longer have dominion over us because we are no longer under the law but under grace.

For Christ is the end of the law for righteousness to everyone who believes. (Romans 10:4)

Do we believe? Then Christ is the end of the law for righteousness to us. Not the end of the law as part of God's Word. Not the end of the law as part of the history of the culture of Israel. But the end of the law as a means of achieving righteousness with God. This applies to everyone who believes, Jew or Gentile, Protestant or Catholic. If you and I want to be reckoned righteous with God by the death of Jesus on the cross, it means the end of the law.

WHEN YOU AND I DISARM THE ENEMY USING THE CROSS AS OUR WEAPON, WE WILL FIND A PLACE OF ULTIMATE SECURITY—A PLACE ON THE OTHER SIDE OF THE CROSS. THAT SECURITY COMES AS WE MAKE A COMMITMENT TO GOD TO GO HIS WAY. IT COMES AS WE DENY OURSELVES, TAKE UP OUR CROSS, AND FOLLOW JESUS.

It is the work of the cross in us that continues to enforce Christ's victory over Satan today. It is the only way for us to resist the evil of this age and the pressures placed upon us by the current society of this world.

But we must apply it daily to receive our full deliverance. You and I can apply the cross in our lives. We can be delivered from this evil age—from the law, from self, from the flesh, and from the world.

STEPPING INTO VICTORY

As we apply the cross in our lives, we can disarm Satan. When you and I disarm the enemy using the cross as our weapon, we will find a place of ultimate security—a place on the other side of the cross. That security comes as we make a commitment to God to go His way. It comes as we deny ourselves, take up our cross, and follow Jesus.

Will you commit yourself to do what Jesus said? Will you deny yourself? Will you take up your cross? Will you follow Him?

If this is your desire, let's express it together with the following prayer. Then, in the last chapter, we will seal this prayer with a powerful confession and proclamation.

Dear Lord, I want to be used by You to bring defeat to the devil and all his agents. Thank You for delivering me through the work Jesus Christ has done on the cross, bringing my release from all forms of witchcraft, from this evil age, and from my own sinful tendencies.

By faith, I step into the freedom Jesus has bought for me. I stand in His authority against all the works of the enemy—in my life and in the world around me.

You are my Lord and Master, and I am Your willing servant. In these significant days, empower me to step into the battle and win the victory in the name of Jesus. Amen.

TWENTY-ONE

SEALING OUR PRAYER

Now, let's affirm our prayer with the following confession and proclamation:

CONFESSION FOR OVERCOMERS

My body is a temple for the Holy Spirit, redeemed, cleansed, and sanctified by the blood of Jesus. My members, the parts of my body, are instruments of righteousness, yielded to God for His service and for His glory. The devil has no place in me, no power over me, no unsettled claim against me. All has been settled by the blood of Jesus. I overcome Satan by the blood of the Lamb and by the word of my testimony, and I love not my life unto the death. My body is for the Lord, and the Lord is for my body. Amen.

PROCLAMATION TO OVERCOME THE DEVIL

I testify to Satan personally as to what the **word** says the **blood** does for me:

Through the blood of Jesus, I am redeemed out of the hand of the devil.

Through the blood of Jesus, all my sins are forgiven.

The blood of Jesus Christ, God's Son, continually cleanses me from all sin.

Through the blood of Jesus, I am justified, made righteous, just-as-if-I'd never sinned.

Through the blood of Jesus, I am sanctified, made holy, set apart to God.

My body is a temple of the Holy Spirit, redeemed, cleansed, by the blood of Jesus.

Satan has no place in me, no power over me, through the blood of Jesus!

ABOUT THE AUTHOR

Derek Prince (1915–2003) was born in India of British parents. He was educated as a scholar of Greek and Latin at Eton College and King's College, Cambridge, in England. Upon graduation, he held a fellowship (equivalent to a professorship) in Ancient and Modern Philosophy at King's College. Prince also studied Hebrew, Aramaic, and modern languages at Cambridge and the Hebrew University in Jerusalem. As a student, he was a philosopher and a self-proclaimed agnostic.

While serving in the Royal Army Medical Corps (RAMC) during World War II, Prince began to study the Bible as a philosophical work. Converted through a powerful encounter with Jesus Christ, he was baptized in the Holy Spirit a few days later. Out of this encounter, he formed two conclusions: first, that Jesus Christ is alive; second, that the Bible is a true, relevant, up-to-date book. These conclusions altered the whole course of his life, which he then devoted to studying and teaching the Bible as the Word of God.

Discharged from the army in Jerusalem in 1945, he married Lydia Christensen, founder of a children's home there. Upon their marriage, he immediately became father to Lydia's eight adopted daughters—six Jewish, one Palestinian Arab, and one English. Together, the family saw the rebirth of the state of Israel in 1948. In the late 1950s, they adopted another daughter while Prince was serving as principal of a teachers' training college in Kenya.

In 1963, the Princes immigrated to the United States and pastored a church in Seattle. In 1973, Prince became one of the founders of Intercessors for America. His book *Shaping History through Prayer and Fasting* has awakened Christians around the world to their responsibility to pray for their governments. Many consider underground translations of the book as instrumental in the fall of communist regimes in the USSR, East Germany, and Czechoslovakia.

Lydia Prince died in 1975, and Prince married Ruth Baker (a single mother to three adopted children) in 1978. He met his second wife, like his first wife, while she was serving the Lord in Jerusalem. Ruth died in December 1998 in Jerusalem, where they had lived since 1981.

Until a few years before his own death in 2003 at the age of eighty-eight, Prince persisted in the ministry God had called him to as he traveled the world, imparting God's revealed truth, praying for the sick and afflicted, and sharing his prophetic insights into world events in the light of Scripture. Internationally recognized as a Bible scholar and spiritual patriarch, Derek Prince established a teaching ministry that spanned six continents and more than sixty years. He is the author of more than eighty books, six hundred audio teachings, and one hundred video teachings, many of which have been translated and published in more than one hundred languages. He pioneered teaching on such groundbreaking themes as generational curses, the biblical significance of Israel, and demonology.

Prince's radio program, which began in 1979, has been translated into more than a dozen languages and continues to touch lives. Derek Prince's main gift of explaining the Bible and its teachings in a clear and simple way has helped build a foundation of faith in millions of lives. His nondenominational, nonsectarian approach has made his teaching equally relevant and helpful to people from all racial and religious backgrounds, and his messages are estimated to have reached more than half the globe.

In 2002, he said, "It is my desire—and I believe the Lord's desire—that this ministry continue the work, which God began through me over sixty years ago, until Jesus returns."

Derek Prince Ministries continues to reach out to believers in over 140 countries with Derek's teaching, fulfilling the mandate to keep on "until Jesus returns." This is accomplished through the outreaches of more than forty-five Derek Prince offices around the world, including primary work in Australia, Canada, China, France, Germany, the Netherlands, New Zealand, Norway, Russia, South Africa, Switzerland, the United Kingdom, and the United States.

For current information about these and other worldwide locations, visit www.derekprince.org.

Welcome to Our House!

We Have a Special Gift for You

It is our privilege and pleasure to share in your love of Christian books. We are committed to bringing you authors and books that feed, challenge, and enrich your faith.

To show our appreciation, we invite you to sign up to receive a specially selected **Reader Appreciation Gift**, with our compliments. Just go to the Web address at the bottom of this page.

God bless you as you seek a deeper walk with Him!

WE HAVE A GIFT FOR YOU. VISIT:

whpub.me/nonfictionthx

WHITAKER
HOUSE